JESUS HOPE

Stephen Travis

Inter-Varsity Press

Inter-Varsity Press
38 De Montfort Street, Leicester LE1 7GP, England

© *Stephen H Travis 1974*

First published 1974
This edition 1980

British Library Cataloguing in Publication Data
   Travis, Stephen
   The Jesus Hope.
   1. Second Advent
   I. Title
   232.6   BT886

   ISBN 0-85110-421-5

Printed and bound in Great Britain by Richard Clay (The Chaucer
Press) Ltd., Bungay, Suffolk.

*Inter-Varsity Press is the publishing division of the Universities and
Colleges Christian Fellowship (formerly the Inter-Varsity Fellowship)
a student movement linking Christian Unions in universities and
colleges throughout the British Isles, and a member movement of the
International Fellowship of Evangelical Students. For information
about local and national activities in Great Britain write to UCCF, 38
De Montfort Street, Leicester LE1 7GP.*

CONTENTS

FOREWORD

The events of the past few years have forced the eyes of all mankind to turn towards the future. Anarchists work to destroy the present structures of society in the hope of bringing in a better world. Communists work and wait for true Socialism to arrive. The 'Men are like gods' school celebrates man's coming of age and looks for the achievements of his maturity. Many ecologists, on the other hand, are less optimistic about the future of *homo sapiens*, and believe that we are so recklessly misusing our non-renewable resources and increasing our population that the future for our world is bleak – if it has a future at all.

Rarely in all these discussions is the distinctively Christian voice heard. Christians appear to be inescapably intertwined with the past – while the rest of mankind is passionately concerned about the future. It comes, therefore, as a surprise to discover that the Christian faith has a great deal to say about the future. And it is not blind speculation, but is based on the teaching, character, death and resurrection of Jesus of Nazareth. Christians believe that the key to understanding the future lies with Jesus, the figure who above all others has dominated the history and culture of the last nineteen hundred years.

Is such a view unrealistic? Does it make sense? Is there any reason to believe it is true? Can we hazard any guesses about the date of history's final chapter? Can we outline any programme? These are among the questions to which Stephen Travis addresses himself in this book. And he is well equipped to do so.

In the first place, he is a scholar of high calibre. He knows the intricate subject of eschatology, or the Last Things, very well. Indeed, his Cambridge doctoral studies were partly in this area. Nevertheless, he manages to write simply and directly, avoiding technical jargon and making profound thoughts readily intelligible through the clarity of his expression.

Second, he is an accomplished writer. He has the gift of making language live, the eye for telling illustrative material, and with it all a practical concern – that our understanding of Then should determine our way of life Now.

Thirdly, he writes with an astonishingly mature judgment. It is easy to be perplexed by the vast range of written material on this subject, or to be beguiled by one of the many conflicting programmes for the End Time. But Dr Travis picks his way skilfully through the jungle of opinions, avoids literalism as well as scepticism, assesses symbolism coolly and sympathetically, and always brings before his readers the main thrust of the biblical material with delicacy and perspective.

I expect to see many more books from Stephen Travis's fluent, scholarly, mature pen. But they will have to be good to better this one. I know of no intellectually respectable treatment of the Second Coming of Christ on the market at present, which is as readable, as relevant and as balanced as this book.

MICHAEL GREEN

PREFACE

This is a book about hope. In days when hope is in short supply, I am persuaded that belief in the biblical promise of the Return of Jesus Christ is the only realistic way to face the future. This hope is not wishful thinking, because it is based on the character of Jesus himself as the Revealer of God. Nor is it escapism. On the contrary, this hope is a powerful motive for positive Christian living and for social change. I have tried throughout the book, and especially in the last three chapters, to show how the Christian hope is not a matter for tickling our minds but for changing our lives and for influencing society.

I would like to thank my colleagues and students at St John's College, Nottingham, for allowing me to try out on them some of the ideas contained in the book. I am especially grateful to Canon Michael Green, who has displayed characteristic generosity in offering advice and encouragement, and in contributing a Foreword.

Each chapter is followed by suggestions for further reading (the more difficult books are marked with an asterisk), and questions for discussion. I hope readers will use these either for personal reflection or group study. In each case there are three discussion questions and one biblical passage suggested for study. As my goal in writing has been to explain the Bible's teaching, so my desire is that through their own study readers may understand more fully the Christian hope and its relevance for daily living.

Old Testament quotations are from the *New English Bible*; New Testament quotations are from *Good News for Modern Man* (*Today's English Version*).

STEPHEN TRAVIS

1

WORLD WITHOUT HOPE?

'But there's got to be hope', cries Mary in the film *On the Beach*. A nuclear war has wiped out civilization in the northern hemisphere, and radioactive dust is drifting southwards, inexorably dealing out to all men radiation sickness, death and oblivion. The film tells how Mary, her husband Peter, and other Australians on the coast of Victoria live out these last doom-filled months before the End. One comforts herself in alcohol, others take reckless risks to win a motor race. Some pack as much pleasure-seeking into the time as they can. Others continue their daily routine as before, resigned to the inevitable. And open-air religious crusades hold the attention of thousands. For Mary's sake, Peter plants trees and buys a rustic garden seat in a charade of hope that somehow there will be a future for themselves and their baby Jennifer. 'There's got to be hope.' But if there isn't, what then?

Visions of the future

Today, hope is in short supply. In previous centuries, when visionaries drew their pictures of the future, they usually described an earthly paradise where everyone's needs were supplied and war was a thing of the past. But most twentieth century prophets are prophets of doom, not of hope – we need think only of George Orwell's *1984*, Aldous Huxley's *Brave New World*, Anthony Burgess's *A Clockwork Orange*, and Neville Shute's *On the Beach*, on which the film was based. To declare glumly that the human situation is getting progressively worse is of course to over-simplify the problem. After all, people have been lamenting man's decline for a long time. It was Aristotle, before 300 B.C., who is supposed to have said, 'When I look at the younger generation, I despair of the future of civilization'. In 1806 William Pitt declared, 'There is nothing around us but ruin and despair'. And in 1892 the Duke of Wellington could write, 'I thank God I shall be spared the consummation of ruin that is gathering around us'.

The fact is that we have got better – and worse. We don't make children work down the mines any more, but we put old people away in homes so that they don't make too many demands on us. But the twentieth century's technological progress has been so rapid that the possibilities both for good and for chaos and destruction are quite different from what they ever were before. The rate of change and development is frightening. My parents were born at a time when few men owned a motor car and few had seen an aeroplane. When I was born aeroplanes were about to drop the first atomic bombs on Hiroshima and Nagasaki. When I was twenty-five I was one of 723 million TV viewers watching Neil Armstrong step onto the moon. Today's children watch a moon-landing as nonchalantly as if it were another episode of *Startrek* – and complain that *Startrek* is more interesting.

If we pause to ask where this rapid rate of change is leading us, the answer is not obvious. It is as though the human race were passengers in an accelerating jet airliner – with no one on the flight deck. In 1973 Professor J. Bronowski presented an impressive series of TV programmes on *The Ascent of Man*. What intrigued me was the built-in assumption of the title. For the higher man ascends, the more catastrophic may be his fall. The more advanced his inventions are, the more likely will be his self-destruction. We can, perhaps, cope with the possibility of our own extinction – after all, we could be killed by a fall from a ladder or a motor accident. But to contemplate the end of the world which produced Plato and Beethoven, Shakespeare and Einstein – that is a prospect from which we recoil.

The results of progress

The prospect, nevertheless, is there to be faced. Consider the following signs of doom. First, there is *the arms race.* Psychiatrist R. D. Laing has calculated that 'normal men have killed perhaps a hundred million of their fellow-men in the last fifty years' [*The Politics of Experience*, 1967, p. 28]. And 'normal men' continue to seek more sophisticated methods of increasing that number. There are countries in South America and Africa which spend more than half their meagre income on 'defence'. The stockpiles of the nuclear powers contain explosives equivalent to a hundred tons of T.N.T. for each inhabitant of the earth. And recent developments in chemical and germ warfare make it perfectly feasible for poorer nations to destroy whole populations of other countries without going to the expense of producing nuclear weapons. There was a time when only God had the power to end the world. Now, it seems, almost anyone can do it.

Then there is *the population crisis.* Although the world's population took two centuries to double between the seventeenth and nineteenth centuries, it is now doubling every thirty-five years. The problem has arisen not because people are producing more babies than they used to, but because medicine and disease-control have dramatically reduced the death rate. And so increasing numbers of people are being preserved by medicine from an early death, in order to face instead the threat of continual starvation.

Population growth puts increasing pressure on *the world's food resources*, as recent price rises indicate. After all, the Indians will not go on indefinitely sending us cheap peanuts for us to nibble with our sherry, while their own people perish for lack of protein. The fact that two-thirds of the human race are living below the breadline is so well known, so often repeated that it raises no more eyebrows than the news that a Hartlepool mid-field player is unfit for Saturday's game. Improved strains of cereals and extensive use of fertilizers can help to increase food supplies, but few experts are confident that supply will keep up with demand for long.

Supplies of *other natural resources*, such as oil, metals and water, are not limitless. It is not only the 'conservation-fanatics' who are warning about this – now even industrialists and governments may be seen head-in-hands with anxieties over shortage of raw materials. And every motorist knows how quickly the price of his petrol has doubled. Western industrial man demands more and more of these resources to feed his technological miracles, and their appetites are insatiable. In the United States a child is born every twelve seconds, a car every five seconds. To keep the car industry growing, cars need to be reasonably rust-prone, and so the world's available metal is being used up with prodigal enthusiasm. And when each car gets on the road it demands its share of petrol. World consumption of petrol doubles every ten years, so that there is not likely to be any left in fifty years' time.

By then, of course, nuclear power may be safe enough to replace oil as a source of energy. But there is no guarantee of our lasting that long, since we might run out of oxygen before then. A car travelling 625 miles uses up as much oxygen as a man breathes in a year; a Boeing 747 burns up fifty tons of oxygen in a single Atlantic crossing. Already the United States produces only sixty per cent of the oxygen it consumes, and if we go on polluting the oceans and thereby killing the oxygen-producing sea-plants, we could reach the stage where there is no longer enough oxygen to support human life. Then man will be like a beast of prey who runs out of victims – and starves to death.

Pollution is a further result of the onward march of technology. Not only do we litter the earth with indestructible plastics and pollute the oceans with sewage and chemicals, we also threaten our own species. On 16th September 1973 a man committed suicide near Kumamoto, Japan, by throwing himself in front of an express train. He had been suffering from mercury poisoning caused by discharge of the metal into Minamata Bay. Also in Japan, the Welfare Ministry estimates that some 340,000 people are still suffering from lingering illnesses caused by atomic fall-out from the bomb dropped on Hiroshima in 1945. Even the peaceful use of nuclear power has its dangers. A 1,000 megawatt nuclear power station produces each year 150 gallons of radioactive liquid waste, which must be kept sealed for two or three hundred years. That is a long time to provide guarantees against accident.

Meanwhile human life continues. But it is life like the life of villagers dwelling in the shadow of a volcano which may erupt at any moment. Former United Nations Secretary General U Thant has said: 'Mankind must find global solutions to global problems or perish − if not with the bang of a nuclear holocaust, then with the whimper of a species in a civilization which ran out of water, resources and food.' And what has caused our arrival at the edge of disaster? Not technology, but what Lewis Mumford has called 'unimproved man'. When he was American Secretary of Defence in the late nineteen-sixties Robert McNamara declared in a speech that the nature of man himself is at the heart of the critical issues of our times. 'All the evidence of history suggests that man is indeed a rational animal, but with a nearly infinite capacity for folly. . . . He draws blueprints for Utopia but never quite gets it built' [quoted in G. Reid, *The Elaborate Funeral*, 1972, p. 48]. Another writer has expressed it like this:

'Creation in Reverse'

'In the end, man destroyed the heaven that had been called earth. For the earth had been beautiful and happy until the destructive spirit of man had moved upon it. This was the seventh day before the end.

For man said ,"Let me have power in the earth", and he saw that the power seemed good and he called those who sought power "great leaders", and those who sought to serve others and bring reconciliation "weaklings", "compromisers", "appeasers". And this was the sixth day before the end.

And man said, "Let there be a division among all people and divide the nations which are for me from the nations which are against me". And this was the fifth day before the end.

And man said, "Let us gather our resources in one place and create more instruments of power and defend ourselves — the radio to control men's minds, conscription to control men's bodies; uniforms and symbols of power to win men's souls". And this was the fourth day before the end.

And man said, "Let there be censorship to divide the propaganda from the truth". And he made two great censorship bureaux to control the thoughts of men – one to tell only the truth he wishes to know at home, the other to tell only the truth that he wishes to know abroad. And this was the third day before the end.

And man said, "Let us create weapons which can kill vast numbers, even millions and hundreds of millions at a distance". And so he perfected germ warfare and deadly underwater arsenals, guided missiles, great fleets of war planes and destructive power to the extent of tens of thousands of millions of tons of T.N.T. And it was the second day before the end.

And man said, "Let us make God in our own image. Let us say God does as we do, thinks as we think, wills as we will, and kills as we kill". So man found ways to kill with atomic power and dust, even those as yet unborn. And he said, "This is necessary. There is no alternative. This is God's will."

And on the last day, there was a great noise upon the face of the earth, and man and all his doings were no more. And the ravished earth rested on the seventh day . . .'

'Hope springs eternal'

Yet few men can live without hope. The child muses about what he wants to be when he grows up, the parent plans for his child's future and his own retirement. The reason why children are captivated by fairy stories and adults by romantic musicals is that their 'Happily ever after' motif expresses something which we all long for and strive for. Without something to look forward to our personalities disintegrate. Buzz Aldrin, the second man to step onto the moon's surface, suffered from mental depression in the year following his Apollo 11 moon mission. In his book *Return to Earth* he describes how he had spent most of his life competing for difficult goals. Now with his moon walk – 'the most important goal of all' – behind him, he suffered from 'the melancholy of all things done'. Feelings of emptiness and meaninglessness are experienced by thousands who have achieved the goals they set themselves, and now have no further to go. And therefore if we are told that the planet earth itself may have no further to go, our sanity is at risk. So what happens then?

There was a time when the Christian hope of Christ's return was a goal to look forward to. It provided assurance that ultimately good would triumph and God's purposes would be achieved, as well as a stimulus to personal devotion, evangelism and social action. But today that hope is widely abandoned. Discredited by the fanatical and disbelieved by the respectable, the message that Christ will come to draw history to a climax has been ignored by preachers and mocked by cartoonists. But if you cast out one supposed demon and offer nothing to take its place, you will find that before long seven others have moved into the empty house. And so it has proved.

Seven substitutes for hope

The first 'demon' to move into the house left vacant by Christian hope is *despair*. If you reject the idea that God has a plan for the world, despair is the only realistic attitude to adopt. A Cambridge student, immersed in the literature of despair and oppressed by the prospect that man might pollute himself into extinction, heard a Christian view of the future explained during a Christian Union mission. She exclaimed afterwards, 'I never thought Christians could be so deluded. Surely you don't *really* believe there is hope?'

The note of despair has often been sounded in pop music. Joan Baez' *Hitchhikers' Song* warns

'You are the orphans in an age of no tomorrows'.

David Bowie's song *Five Years* catches the horror of knowing that time is running out:

'Pushing through the market square, so many mothers sighing.
News had just come over, we had five years left to cry in.
News guy wept when he told us, earth was really dying –
Cried so much his face was wet, then I knew he was not lying. . . .
We got five years, my brain hurts a lot.
We got five years, that's all we got.'

What the young sing at their pop festivals, old men utter as the considered wisdom of their advancing years. In 1955, two days before Albert Einstein died, he and Bertrand Russell delivered a 'Manifesto' in London. Describing the risks of thermonuclear war, they claimed, 'We have found that the men who know most are the most gloomy'. Russell's own view of the world was expressed in his poignant words: 'Only on the firm foundation of unyielding despair can the soul's habitation be safely built'.

But today pop music shows fewer signs of black despair, and genuinely pessimistic people are hard to find, because our hearts cry out for goals to achieve and dreams to fulfil. And so a more popular substitute for hope is the *bland optimism* which smacks more of wishful thinking than of serious grappling with available evidence. In a BBC *Controversy* programme in September 1973, the well-known 'futurologist' Hermann Kahn presented the case for optimism. In a hundred years or so, he suggested, we could expect a world population of 15,000,000,000, with each family owning three houses, two cars and perhaps a submarine. He admitted that probably seventy major world problems would crop up in the next ten or twenty years, but 'given moderately reasonable behaviour' the human race would survive to enjoy his projected utopia. With optimists like that, who needs pessimists? What confidence does history give us that humanity can face seventy major problems and approach each one reasonably? Such optimism fails miserably to come to terms with the power of evil. Of course, we all hope that 'somehow we'll get through'. But this kind of secular optimism is an enemy, not an ally, of real Christian hope, because it does nothing about the problem of evil.

Thirdly there is *escapism*. In 1968 a *Life* magazine reporter brought news of Robert Kennedy's assassination to groups of young Americans who had opted out of the complexities of modern life and were living in caves at Matalo in Crete. Their response to the news was — silence. 'No shock, no rage, no tears. Is this the new phenomenon? Running away from America *and* running away from emotions? I understand uninvolvement, disenchantment, even non-commitment, but where has all the feeling gone?' That was their way of coping with the crisis. Others seek escape in some form of mysticism. To Zen Buddhists and Hindu gurus, to ouija boards and black magic rites they go in search of inner peace and security – something to shield them from the uncomforting grimness of reality.

Yet others escape not to mysticism but to the past. The craze for antique furniture, the waiting list of 24,000 for a seat in the audience of the BBC's *Good Old Days*, the longing we feel that things and places should remain as they were in our childhood – all these reflect what Alvin Toffler calls 'the psychological lust for the simpler, less turbulent past'.

A fourth way of coping with crisis is in a *trip of self-indulgence* – the time-honoured method of 'Let us eat, drink and be merry, for tomorrow we die'. Many of the great civilizations of history have collapsed amid an orgy of entertainment which kept from people's minds the thought of imminent catastrophe. Never has the entertainment industry been so huge as it is today, and never so readily available as on TV. So if the news is disturbing, we know it will be followed by *The Generation Game* or *Starsky and Hutch*. And if there's a programme about politics or pollution, we can always switch over to *Hawaii-Five-O*. For there's a limit to how much reality our emotions can face. Not that there's anything wrong with some good entertainment, of course. It's all a matter of degree.

While some are content to be hypnotized into passive observance of TV shows, others seek out experiences which will bring some satisfaction in the time before the End. The dare-devil riding of the ton-up boys in the early sixties, and the more recent prominence of experiments with drugs and sex – these are the last wriggle in the tail of a generation which doubts whether it has a future. We are the 'Now generation', for whom the past is irrelevant and the future totally uncertain.

A fifth substitute-hope is *astrology*. Finding no security in traditional religion, thousands turn to astrologers for guidance. In Britain one woman astrologer claims that forty well-known businessmen consult her before taking major policy decisions. In the United States 1,200 of the country's 1,750 daily papers carry a column of horoscopes, and there are reported to be 10,000 professional astrologers. In the week when I wrote this chapter, the *Radio Times* carried an advert offering free full-colour horoscope books to all buyers of Radiomobile car radios. A few years ago I met a fellow-student carrying a publication called *Your Future in the Stars*. When I asked him whether he took it seriously he replied in all innocence, 'Why not?' And yet you only have to read your horoscope in a few newspapers on the same day, and you find that they are either so vague as to be useless, or so contradictory as to be ridiculous. But astrology increasingly fascinates people, supposedly helping them to manipulate the future for their own benefit. And isn't this basically selfish? – you never find the stars telling you to 'take up your cross'.

Sixthly, there is *the goal of the totalitarian state*. Having removed religion as a source of hope, both Fascism and Communism have created the goal of a national utopia. 'We have created our myth', declared Mussolini at Naples in 1922. 'The myth is a faith, it is a passion. It is not necessary that it shall be a reality. It is a reality by the fact that it is a goad, a hope, a faith, that it is courage. Our myth is the nation.' And the followers of Marx are inspired by a vision of a future classless society where all men are equal and all needs are met. Meanwhile the value of the individual is sacrificed to the interests of the state, and the citizens of these countries 'on the way to utopia' are kept inside by machine-guns and barbed-wire fences. The path to paradise has been blown apart by the Communist leaders' failure to acknowledge the realities of human nature either in themselves or in their subjects.

Finally, there is the *radical idealism* of young people, especially students, in the free world. Rightly they have protested about the futility of war and the rape of the environment. Rightly they have denounced our capitalist society's lack of compassion towards the poor and oppressed. But for two reasons they have failed to see their hopes fulfilled. First, their revolutionary programme was inadequate. Seeing keenly the weaknesses of western society, they failed to offer an adequate alternative. Interviewed in *Playboy* in 1969, Mick Jagger of the Rolling Stones saw this. Although advocating some kind of revolution, he admitted, 'I've got no alternative society I'd like to set up. . . . O.K., you can say: Right, no queen, no parliament; but how much difference would it make in the end? Maybe you'll end up by banning dancing, like Cromwell. So what? The worst thing wrong with this country is that there *were* certain values here and now there's so many people trying to sweep values away. . . . They sweep away and they've got nothing to sweep back.' And secondly, their increasing resort to violence has precipitated the use of force against them by the society they sought to change. Few of us like to see the police acting tough at a demonstration, but most of us prefer that to the chaotic anarchy which the radicals' programme seems to involve.

Jesus and man's hope

These, then, are seven popular 'philosophies' of our day. Most of them are successful, if numbers are anything to go by. Some of them contain truth. Some deserve admiration and respect. I mention them not to write them off as unworthy of consideration, but because they show that men cannot live without hope.

But have these seven 'philosophies' *changed* anything? Very little. The future of the world remains in doubt because the nature of man remains unchanged. These substitute-hopes only accommodate to human nature. They do not change it. If the politicians and the pop musicians are more optimistic now than they were five years ago, it is not because the situation has improved. It is because hope is a necessity of life. We need a hope which takes seriously the nature of man himself. And to find that, we must look again at the Christian hope. This book explains the conviction that God has acted in Jesus Christ, crucified, risen and exalted. Jesus is the key to hope.

For further reading

*O. Guinness, *The Dust of Death* (IVP, 1973)
*J. W. Sire, *The Universe Next Door* (IVP, 1977)

Questions for Discussion

1. When you look at the world today, are you optimistic or pessimistic about its future? Why?
2. Whose responsibility is it to 'do something' about the 'signs of doom' mentioned in this chapter? Why does it take so long to *get* anything done?
3. Select two or three of the 'substitute-hopes' listed in this chapter, and discuss why people find them attractive, and what their inadequacies are.
4. Study Romans 1: 18-32. How accurately does this describe our own society? According to this passage, how has men's current sinful state come about?

* In the reading lists at the end of each chapter an asterisk denotes the more difficult books.

2

THE BEGINNING OF THE END

When Jesus of Nazareth appeared in Palestine, he came into a world already alive with rival views about the future. There was, for example, the Pharisaic party, which was popular with the middle classes of Judaism. They were hoping for the coming of a warrior-king – a descendant of the great king David – who would drive out the hated Romans and restore the fortunes of Israel. And they believed that by obedience to God's law they could hasten the day when this messiah would appear. The party of the Sadducees, however, which included many of the Jewish religious leaders, did not believe in the resurrection of the dead, and were happy to collaborate with the Romans in order to preserve their privileged positions.

Then there were the Essenes, such as the monks of the Qumran community near the Dead Sea, whose writings have been coming to light since 1947. They so despised the religious compromise of the Jerusalem priesthood that they withdrew to the desert, there to live pure lives in preparation for the coming of God's kingdom. When God's moment came, they would rise up to fight in a final battle between the Sons of Light (themselves) and the Sons of Darkness (almost everyone else). God would give them a glorious victory and so his reign of blessing would begin.

A fourth group was the guerilla movement of the first century, the Zealots. One of Jesus' disciples, Simon 'the Zealot' (Luke 6: 15), had belonged to this group, and possibly Judas Iscariot did too. Their plan was to overthrow the Romans by armed revolt, so that God's kingdom of peace and justice could be established in Palestine. During the first century several of their armed revolutions were squashed by the might of Rome, and their leaders were crucified as a grim deterrent from further revolt.

God's rule has begun!

All four of these hopes have echoes in the twentieth century. None of them is the way of Jesus. When he began his ministry in Palestine he must have known of their existence, and he rejected them all. He denounced the corruption of the religious leaders. He abhorred the legal wrangles by which men sidestepped the demands of love. He lived in the midst of men, not cut off from them in a monastery. He rejected the chance of violent revolution when his admirers clamoured for it. And he declared that the God-sent deliverer would be a spiritual leader, not a military one. But that was not all.

Luke's Gospel records the dramatic scene when Jesus went at the outset of his ministry to the synagogue in his home town of Nazareth (Luke 4: 16–30). He was invited to read from Isaiah 61 a passage which looks forward to the day when God would draw near to his people and establish his kingdom of justice, peace and liberation:

'The Spirit of the Lord is upon me.
He has anointed me to preach the Good News to the poor,
He has sent me to proclaim liberty to the captives,
And recovery of sight to the blind,
To set free the oppressed,
To announce the year when the Lord will save his people!'

Then he closed the book, returned it to the attendant and announced to the congregation: 'This passage of scripture has come true today, as you heard it being read'. That was his message. The day which prophets and dreamers had longed for was here! The promise was fulfilled, a new era had begun!

Jesus called this new era the 'kingdom', or the 'kingly reign' of God. The term does not mean a slice of land or a social order. It means God ruling in people's lives, bringing them his blessings. It means that God's programme of liberation is no longer reserved for the remote future, it has already begun. The coming of Jesus is the beginning of hope.

On one occasion the imprisoned John the Baptist sent a message to Jesus, anxiously asking, 'Are you the one John said was going to come, or should we expect someone else?' Back from Jesus went the reassuring reply: 'Go back and tell John what you have seen and heard: the blind can see, the lame can walk, the lepers are made clean, the deaf can hear, the dead are raised to life, and the Good News is preached to the poor' (Luke 7: 18–23). He was in fact quoting from Isaiah 35, to show that the blessings expected by the prophet in God's future kingdom were now happening, in Jesus' actions! Where Jesus is, the power of God's reign is already at work. It is like new wine, so fresh and potent that old wine-skins can't contain it (Mark 2: 22). What Jesus brought was not just a new teaching, but a new event, a new power. It was a real foretaste of God's ultimate plan for man and his world.

The reign of a Father

What did Jesus say about God's reign? The high note of his message was that the king whose reign has begun is not a stern and distant ruler, but a Father. He taught his followers to pray, 'Our Father . . .'. But there's something we must be clear about. The idea of God as Father is so familiar to us that we are apt to assume that the Fatherhood of God was the message Jesus proclaimed to all and sundry.

Far from it. When Jesus spoke to God, he used a word from his native Aramaic – 'Abba' (Mark 14: 36). This was a term of endearment which any child would use in addressing his father. It means 'dear father', or even 'daddy'. No Jew would dare to address the high and holy God like this. Jesus was the first to do so. Yet if you look in the earliest Gospel, Mark, you will find that only very rarely does Jesus speak of God as Father. He did so only to a chosen few and in private.

The reason is that the experience of God as Father was the greatest and deepest reality of his life. And we don't speak lightly to all and sundry about the things that are most deeply precious to us. Jesus had a profound conviction of being in a very special relationship with God. And, amazingly, he said that those who attach themselves to him may share – as a sheer gift of God's love – this kind of relationship with God as Father: 'My Father has given me all things. No one knows the Son except the Father, and no one knows the Father except the Son, and those to whom the Son wants to reveal him' (Matthew 11:27). 'When you have committed yourself to me', Jesus was saying, 'then you can call God Father.' And what kind of Father is he? He is one who actively seeks out men and welcomes them into friendship with him – like the father in the story of the prodigal son, running to welcome his son home (Luke 15).

God's reign in action

As the bringer of God's reign, Jesus offers forgiveness of sins. His very name, Jesus, means that: 'God to the rescue!' (Matthew 1:21). He created a stir at Capernaum when he declared to a paralysed man, 'My son, your sins are forgiven' (Mark 2:5). 'Blasphemy!', murmured the religious experts. 'Who can forgive sins but God alone?' They were quite right – unless of course Jesus was speaking in God's name. And to show that there need be no doubt about that, he raised the paralysed man from his bed and sent him away healed.

Jesus did not bring a new teaching about forgiveness, he offered men a new experience of forgiveness. He went for the down-and-outs, the despised tax-collectors and prostitutes, removed from them the stains of the past and offered fresh hope for the future. And when the critics mumbled about how unseemly it all was, he told them about a shepherd who went out in search of a lost sheep, until he brought it home rejoicing. And about a housewife who lost a pound note and when eventually she found it she called in all the neighbours to share her joy. 'Just so, I tell you, there is joy before the angels of God over one sinner who repents' (Luke 15: 10).

This has been the experience of millions ever since. Blatant sinners like Mary Magdalene, respectable sinners like Saul of Tarsus, ordinary sinners like most of us – all may hear these words, 'Your sins are forgiven'. But it is only for those who are willing to turn from wrong and receive it. Most of us are prepared to agree that the cause of most of the world's troubles is the evil in men's hearts. But we find it rather difficult to admit to our own guilt. Few are as honest as C. S. Lewis who tells how 'for the first time I examined myself with a serious practical purpose. And there I found what appalled me: a zoo of lusts, a bedlam of ambitions, a nursery of fear, a hareem of fondled hatreds. My name was legion.' But that was the prelude to his being 'surprised by joy'. This is the kingdom of God in action: God drawing near to forgive the evil in our hearts and to establish his reign within us.

A further point is that God's reign concerns man's whole personality. If the forgiveness of sins shows that God's reign has begun, so do Jesus' healings and exorcisms. When his Pharisaic opponents disputed the source of his power to exorcise demons, Jesus rounded on them. 'No', he said, 'it is God's Spirit who gives me the power to drive out demons, which proves that the kingdom of God has already come upon you.' And when John the Baptist's message came asking if he was the expected messiah, Jesus pointed to what God was doing through him – 'the blind can see, the lame can walk, the lepers are made clean, the deaf can hear, the dead are raised to life, and the Good News is preached to the poor' (Luke 7: 22).

God is not concerned only with men's spiritual needs, but with physical needs too. He is concerned with the whole man. And Jesus' miracles of healing are signs that ultimately he will triumph over all the forces which make men less than whole. Jesus' Good News is meant to make us into new men, transformed at every level.

Evil defeated

Jesus' bringing of God's reign was no easy-going thing. It was a battle. At the beginning of his ministry he endured a period of intense temptation (Matthew 4: 1–11). Constantly he encountered the dark spiritual forces which twist and stunt men's lives. 'No one', he declared, 'can break into a strong man's house and take away his belongings unless he ties up the strong man first; then he can plunder his house' (Matthew 11: 29). But that's just what Jesus was doing – overpowering the forces of evil and plundering their territory, claiming men for God. When his followers returned from a preaching and healing mission to tell how they had exorcised the demon-possessed, Jesus exclaimed: 'I saw Satan fall like lightning from heaven' (Luke 10: 18). Confronted by the advance of God's reign, the forces of evil are on the run.

We are often told these days that it's naïve to believe in the devil and all that primitive nonsense. But when I hear of the colossal resurgence of witchcraft, devil-worship and spiritism, I wonder who it is who's being naïve. Nevertheless, Jesus persistently conquered in his encounters with evil, and his followers share his victory. In the New Testament it is not believers who tremble at the power of Satan, but demons who tremble at the power of God (James 2: 19).'

Christ's conflict with evil had its climax in the cross. '*Now* the ruler of this world will be overthrown', he said as he approached his death on the cross (John 12: 31). And 'Finished! ' was his triumphant shout before he died (John 19: 30). The forces of evil had done their worst, and failed.

'And on that cross Christ freed himself from the power
of the spiritual rulers and authorities; he made a public
spectacle of them by leading them as captives in his victory
procession' (Colossians 2: 15).

A new people of God

The very idea of God's reign implies that the king
has subjects! When we turn to the Gospels we find Jesus
choosing twelve men and sharing his purpose with them.
What breathtaking cheek! Twelve was the number of the
tribes of Israel. And Jesus was implying that his twelve
disciples were to be the nucleus of a new Israel, a new
people of God. In due course he sent out the twelve to
proclaim the Good News of God's reign (Matthew 10).
Why? To call others into the new community.

And when Jesus held the Last Supper, he was establishing his church as a continuing community. 'This is my
body which is broken for you. . . . This cup is the *new
covenant* in my blood' (1 Corinthians 11: 24f). 1,200 years
previously, at Sinai, God had formed the Israelites into a
people of God by making a 'covenant' – a relationship –
with them. Now on the eve of his death Jesus was making
a New Covenant, forming a new people of God.

Jesus' parable of the tenants in the vineyard takes this
point further. A landowner rented his vineyard to tenants
and left home on a trip. When he sent servants to collect
the product of the grape harvest the tenants attacked them,
killing some and injuring others. At last he sent his son.
'Surely they will respect my son', he said. But when the
tenants saw the son they reasoned, 'This is the owner's son.
Come on, let's kill him, and we shall get his property! ' So
they grabbed him and killed him. 'What would the owner
do then? ' asked Jesus. 'He will punish them of course, and
rent the vineyard out to other tenants, who will give him
his share of the harvest at the right time.' And as the
hearers were murmuring their approval of Jesus' wisdom,
he drove home the point: 'The kingdom of God will be

taken away from you and be given to a people who will produce the proper fruits.'

No wonder Matthew adds the comment: 'The chief priests and the Pharisees heard Jesus' parables and knew that he was talking about them, so they tried to arrest him' (Matthew 21: 33–44). For he was striking at the very roots of their religion. 'You are wrong,' he was saying, 'if you imagine that God's purposes are intended only for Jews. He is forming a new people before your eyes, composed of Gentiles as well as Jews. Whether you belong to it depends not on your ancestry but on how you respond to my message about God's reign.'

Ever since, this people has continued to grow. Like the tiny mustard seed which grows into a tree, God's reign extends from small beginnings, until today millions in earth and heaven call God their king.

To call God king involves a new style of living. When Jesus gave the teaching contained in the Sermon on the Mount (Matthew 5–7), he wasn't just giving a new law, more difficult and more demanding than the old one. He was describing what it means to respond to the grace of God who brings his reign near to us. If he says 'You must forgive,' it is because he has already said to us, 'Your sins are forgiven'. If he commands us to love our enemies, it is because we are children of God who 'makes his sun to shine on bad and good people alike, and gives rain to those who do right and those who do wrong' (Matthew 5: 45). Always it is a matter of 'Freely you have received, therefore freely give.'

How different this is from the attitude which says, 'Well, I never do anyone any harm! ' Here is a man who has received so much from others, let alone from God, a man with so much potential for good and self-giving to others. And all he can say is, 'I never do anyone any harm'. What a miserable standard to live by! Jesus challenges men to a new way of life, and he offers something which sets him apart from other ethical teachers: he provides the dynamic to live this kind of life. Now that God's reign has begun,

he pours his love into the hearts of all who will receive it.
He fills them with new attitudes, new ideals, new deter-
mination to express God's love in action.

Good news for all

On a dark Saturday morning last winter a notice appeared
on the main road near where I live. It read: 'NEWS FOR
ALL – DERBY COUNTY MATCH POSTPONED'. The
arrival of God's reign is certainly news for all, and Jesus
was at pains to make this clear. He soon got a reputation
for mixing with the outcasts of society – lepers, beggars,
cheating tax-collectors, a woman discovered in the act of
adultery. He mixed with them not to condone their condition, but to bring near to them the blessings of God's
reign – healing, forgiveness, justice, and a new power for
living.

Jesus' story of the king who gave a wedding feast for
his son illustrates this. When the invited guests refused to
come, he sent his servants out into the streets to gather in
all the people they could find, good and bad alike, till the
wedding hall was filled with people (Matthew 22: 1–10).
Who ever heard of a king pulling people in off the streets
for a party? Exactly. God is like no human king. His kingdom is open to all who will come, Jew or Gentile, down-
and-out or up-and-out.

Jesus did not command his followers to take this message
to all men so much as *assume* that they would. Once he was
having a meal at Bethany, a village tucked behind the
eastern slopes of the Mount of Olives. A woman came in
and as a mark of devotion to him poured a jar of expen-
sive perfume over his head. When other guests criticized
her extravagance Jesus remarked, 'She has done a beautiful
thing for me. She poured perfume on my body to prepare
it for burial ahead of time. Now, remember this! Wherever
the gospel is preached, all over the world, what she has
done will be told in memory of her' (Mark 14: 3–9). In
saying this, Jesus *assumed* that the good news of God's

reign would be carried worldwide. And so it has proved. The Christian message has been proclaimed, the Gospels have been translated into hundreds of languages, and this woman's act of worship is known worldwide.

But although God's reign is for all men, not all men receive it. Jesus doesn't force himself on people. In fact he specifically rejected the way of violent revolution when the opportunity presented itself. After he miraculously fed a crowd of five thousand, they became enthusiastically convinced of his ability to be a warrior-messiah, a leader of armed rebellion. But Jesus, 'knowing that they were about to make him king by force, went off to the hills by himself' (John 6: 15).

Jesus didn't use armed force, and he doesn't use force of any kind. His only weapon is love. Napoleon is said to have remarked, 'Alexander, Caesar and I have conquered the world by force. But Jesus Christ conquered by love, and still today millions would gladly die for him.'

So there is a choice to be made: to respond to his love or to reject it. Time and again Jesus challenged men to take decisive action if they were to know the blessings of God's reign. 'Remember this!' he urged. 'Unless you change your ways and become humble like little children, you will never enter the kingdom of heaven' (Matthew 18: 3f). And Mark sums up Jesus' whole message in the words, 'The right time has come, and the kingdom of God is near! Turn away from your sins and believe the Good News!' (Mark 1: 15).

The best is yet to come

By his coming, his preaching, his healing, his death and resurrection Jesus brought God's reign near to men. He introduced a new era. He set human history on a new course, he transformed individual human lives. He commissioned his followers to take his Good News to all men, challenging them to enter the kingdom and begin a new relationship with God as Father.

But that is only a beginning. Jesus healed, but people still suffer. He triumphed over evil, but evil's destructive power is still around and within us. He claimed to set free the oppressed, but still men are oppressed through war, hatred, prejudice and vested interests. Why? Because the new era which Jesus introduced was only the 'beginning of the end.' It wasn't God's *final* act of deliverance – that is still to come.

Jesus spoke of a time in the future when God will act to establish his kingdom completely. *Then* evil will be finally conquered and God will rule with love over willing subjects. On that day, Jesus said, 'the Son of Man (Jesus' own favourite title for himself) will appear, coming in the clouds with great power and glory' (Mark 13: 26). Meanwhile, between the first and final comings of Christ, Christians experience the tension between good and evil, love and hate, wholeness and suffering. We are on the journey, but we haven't yet arrived.

But we *are* on the journey, if we have committed ourselves to Christ. And the one who will meet us at the end is not some unknown, fearsome figure, but Jesus. When he left his followers after his resurrection, two angels appeared and asked them, 'Why do you stand there looking up at the sky? This Jesus, who was taken up from you into heaven, will come back in the same way that you saw him go into heaven' (Acts 1: 11). *This Jesus* will come back! So we can face the future with confidence – not because we have a crystal ball in which to see all the details, but because the future is in the hands of one whom we know. That's what makes all the difference. God's plan for the future is to complete what he began when Jesus came. The programme of love and liberation which Jesus announced in the Nazareth synagogue is still in operation. One day it will be complete.

For further reading

*C. H. Dodd, *The Founder of Christianity* (Fontana, 1973)

R. T. France, *The Man They Crucified* (IVP, 1975)

E. M. B. Green, *Jesus Spells Freedom* (IVP, 1972)

Questions for Discussion

1. Suppose Jesus had never come, and his 'good news of the kingdom' had never been proclaimed. What difference would it make to your life?

2. Make a list of the different *kinds* of people whom Jesus welcomed into his kingdom. Is your church in touch with such a wide range of people? If not, what could you do about it?

3. Are there aspects of Jesus' message which are not stressed enough in your church and in your own thinking? What are they?

4. Study Luke 11: 1–13. What does the passage teach about God's fatherly care for his people? Share with each other what these things mean to you personally.

3

SIGNS OF THE TIMES

On my desk is a cartoon showing a man with a placard announcing: 'THE WORLD ENDS TOMORROW'. Beside him is a policeman who says, 'If it doesn't I'm pinching you under the Trade Descriptions Act.'

In what sense is it right to look forward to the return of Christ and the end of human history? Is it right to calculate when the End will be? These questions are asked by many today, and they were asked of Jesus himself by some of his followers. Chapter 13 of Mark's Gospel records Jesus' surprising reply.

Prelude: doom on the temple

As Jesus came out of the temple in Jerusalem, one of his followers remarked about the building's breathtaking beauty. Jesus' devastating reply was that even this magnificent building – for the Jews the place where God's presence was especially to be found – was to be utterly destroyed. 'Not a single stone here will be left in its place, every one of them will be thrown down' (Mark 13: 2). The Jews' rejection of the good news of God's reign sealed their judgment.

On the Mount of Olives, overlooking Jerusalem from the east, there stands today a little church known as 'Jesus Wept'. On the front of the altar is a mosaic depicting a hen with chickens under her wings, and round the mosaic is written in Latin Jesus' words: 'O Jerusalem, Jerusalem. . . . How many times have I wanted to put my arms around all your people, just as a hen gathers her chicks under her wings, but you would not let me! ' (Matthew 23: 37). The church stands there as a witness to the persistent love which led Jesus to weep over a city doomed because it rejected his offer of God's forgiveness.

Later, as Jesus sat on the Mount of Olives overlooking the temple, Peter, Andrew, James and John took the opportunity to ask him about his prediction of doom on the temple. 'Tell us when this will be', they said; 'and tell us what is the sign that will show that it is the time for all these things to happen' (Mark 13: 4). There are actually two questions here: When will the temple be destroyed? And when will the end of the age occur? Peter and his friends assumed that the destruction of Jerusalem – which the Romans achieved in A.D. 70 – was linked with the end of the world. Now they were wrong if they thought that the world would end *at the same time* as the fall of Jerusalem. But they were right to see a *connection* between the destruction of Jerusalem and the end of the world. For in Jesus' reply to the disciples' question, he made it clear that what happened to Jerusalem in A.D. 70 was part of the process of the coming of God's kingdom and his judgment on evil. That is why in Mark 13 the events of A.D. 70 and the events of some future unknown date are woven together.

But how does Jesus reply to their request for a sign to show when the End is near? This is the question which people never tire of asking. 'When will the End be?' they ask. 'Please may we have an infallible means of recognizing that the End is approaching?' It is a very natural question, because a clear answer would satisfy our curiosity and our need for security. It would also relieve us of having to be prepared for Christ's coming at any time.

But it is a question which Jesus refused to answer. He did not give them a 'Sign', but a baffling list of signs. And the signs which he gave are not a futurologist's slide-rule by which you can calculate when the End will be. They are characteristics of *the whole period* between the resurrection of Jesus and his coming again. They are symptoms of the conflict which is raging between good and evil, between God and the armies of Satan. They are signs that the End is on its way, but not signs which enable us to work out God's timetable.

This is where I part company from many writers of recent years who have tried to show that, since all the predictions of Mark 13 and other passages of Scripture are being marvellously fulfilled in our own day, the End of Time is just around the corner. I shall say more about them in chapter seven. But here we can note one problem which their view raises. Certainly the signs which Jesus lists in Mark 13 are visible in our own day – false teaching, wars, famine, persecution and the rest – but they have been constantly visible right through Christian history. That is why we cannot say they are signs in the same sense as the chime of Big Ben tells us that *News at Ten* is about to begin.

No, they are signs which we can expect right through the period from the resurrection of Jesus till his final coming. This whole period is called in the Bible 'the last days'. Peter, for example, in his sermon at Pentecost claimed that the coming of the Holy Spirit was the fulfilment of Joel's prophecy of what God would do 'in the last days' (Acts 2: 16f). So 'the last days' are not the final few years before the return of Jesus, but the whole period from Jesus' resurrection to his final coming, however long that may be.

Characteristics of the last days

Jesus' aim in telling us these signs was not to satisfy our curiosity, but to strengthen faith and warn of dangers that Christians can expect. So what are they?

First, there will be *false messiahs*. 'Many will come in my name, saying, "I am he!"', and fool many people' (Mark 13: 6). From New Testament times to the present day there have been people who falsely claimed to be the Messiah or in some way to represent Jesus. In Autumn

1972, a man calling himself 'The Messiah' was arrested in New Guinea and charged with murder. A few months before, he had set up his own religious cult and gained hypnotic control over several hundred followers. Two of them, both respected farmers, volunteered to have themselves beaten to death on the understanding that they would rise again at midnight. They did not. Others plunged to their deaths from high places clutching Bibles and believing they would rise again. None of 'The Messiah's' promises was kept.

In February 1971 a woman named Edna Ballard, head of the 'I Am' religious movement, died in her Chicago home. The event went unpublicized because the movement doesn't believe in death.

And then there are the modern-day cults – Jehovah's Witnesses, Christadelphians, Mormons and the others. In his book *Christian Deviations* Horton Davies points out errors which most of these cults have in common. His list includes the following:

1. The danger of exaggerating one part of Christian faith at the expense of other parts. Christian Science, for example, does this in its over-emphasis on healing.

2. The danger of over-emphasizing the Old Testament at the expense of the New. Examples of this tendency are Jehovah's Witnesses, Christadelphians, Mormons and Seventh Day Adventists.

3. The danger of seeking for greater assurance in the religious life than Christ actually offers. For instance, there is Spiritism with its attempt to get proof of life after death. And there are all those groups who make confident and detailed predictions of future events.

4. The danger of spiritual arrogance which declares that all who do not belong to this or that sect are 'beyond the pale'.

5. The temptation to use God as a means to an end. Christian Science tends to use God as a convenience for obtaining good health, and Moral Re-Armament regards God as the supreme weapon in defeating Communism.

6. A concentration on 'glory for me', and an opting out of responsibilities towards family and society. The attitude of Jehovah's Witnesses in this respect is well known.

7. The error shared by nearly all these sects is their distortion of the biblical doctrine of Christ. Jesus is regarded as a mere man, rather than as the unique revelation of God.

Why are these sects so successful? One reason is that, unlike the true Messiah, they are not reluctant to show signs and wonders. 'False messiahs and false prophets will appear', Jesus warned. 'They will perform signs and wonders for the purpose of deceiving God's chosen people, if possible' (Mark 13: 12f). They exploit men's natural craving to escape from the uncertainties of faith into the comfortable security of sight.

And they aren't the only ones. Aren't the seven errors listed above sometimes within the Christian communities themselves? All this in spite of Jesus' warning, 'Be on your guard! I have told you everything ahead of time' (Mark 13: 23).

The second mark of the last days is *world conflict and natural disasters*. Wars, earthquakes and famines are not confined to a period immediately before the return of Jesus. They have happened throughout history. And the twentieth century has witnessed no slacking in their intensity. If it is true that we have killed a hundred million of our fellow-men since 1900, it is also true that countless others have died in earthquakes – including 50,000 in Peru in 1970, when we were so busy watching the World Cup on TV that we hardly noticed. And every day ten thousand or more die or starvation – each of them a human being with as much right to a decent life as I have.

When we hear all this it is very easy to feel that God has forgotten his world, and to wonder whether his kingdom of peace will ever come. But Jesus urged, 'Don't be alarmed. These things are like the first pains of childbirth' (Mark 13: 7f). They are the labour pains which herald the joy of birth. They are signs of the conflict between God and the evil forces which are at work in man and the universe. So while they should be cause for deep concern, they should not take us by surprise. That isn't all the Christian faith has to say about wars and disasters, of course, but it's part of the picture.

Thirdly, Jesus promised *persecution for his followers*. There was nothing in *his* teaching about religion being the opium of the people. Far from it. 'Everyone will hate you because of me', he said (Mark 13: 13). 'No slave is greater than his master. If they persecuted me, they will persecute you too' (John 15: 20). This again is part of the conflict between the kingdom of God and the forces opposed to God.

Jesus warned that persecution would come through the official channels of state and religion, and through personal hostility too. Jesus himself knew the pain of being betrayed by one of his close circle of friends, and he knew that the pattern would be repeated. 'Men will hand over their own brothers to be put to death, and fathers will do the same to their children; children will turn against their parents and have them put to death' (Mark 13: 12). Perhaps the hardest thing a Christian can ever face is when members of his own family turn against him and become the agents of his martyrdom. But it has happened, and it will happen again.

But persecution is not all gloom, as God's suffering people have frequently shown. 'You will stand before rulers and kings for my sake, to tell them the Good News', said Jesus (Mark 13: 9). Peter, Stephen and Paul were only the first of countless Christians who have used their trials as opportunities to bear frank and fearless witness to their Lord. And when the crucial time comes, they are promised the help of God. 'The words you speak will not be yours; they will come from the Holy Spirit' (Mark 13: 11). Instead of you defending Christianity, God will defend you! And finally Jesus gave the assurance that 'the person who holds out to the end will be saved' (Mark 13: 13). Testing is a mark of the last days, and perseverance through testing is a mark that your faith is real.

The fourth characteristic of the last days is *world mission*. In the middle of Jesus' warning about persecution comes the promise, 'The gospel must first be preached to all peoples' (Mark 13: 10). This is a promise that the gospel will be preached, not necessarily that it will be believed by all people. But the Bible is full of the great hope that God will draw men of all races to himself. The author of the book of Revelation saw in his vision a great crowd of worshippers in heaven. 'They were from every nation, tribe, people, and language, and they stood in front of the throne and of the Lamb, dressed in white robes, and holding palm branches in their hands. They called out in a loud voice: "Our salvation comes from our God, who sits on the throne, and from the Lamb! " ' (Revelation 7: 9f).

How seriously do we take our involvement in the world mission of the Church? That is a measure of how much we long for the purpose of Christ to be fulfilled and his kingdom to be established.

The destruction of Jerusalem

The fifth sign is *the fall of Jerusalem*. In the central section of Mark 13 Jesus was plainly speaking about a coming catastrophe within history (verses 14–20). 'You will see "the Awful Horror" standing in the place where he should not be', he began (Mark 13: 14). What does this mean? Originally the term 'the Awful Horror' was used in Daniel 12:11 to describe the heathen altar set up in the Jerusalem temple by Antiochus IV Epiphanes, an oppressive Syrian ruler, in 168 B.C. But Jesus used the term to warn that something similar would happen again. When that time came men would be wise to flee to the hills, without delaying even to pick up an overcoat. Pregnant women and those with young children would suffer unimaginable stress. And so it proved in A.D. 70 when the Roman army captured Jerusalem after a few months' siege, butchered thousands and burned down the temple.

After predicting the fall of Jerusalem Jesus went on: 'The trouble of those days will be far worse than anything the world has ever known, from the very beginning when God created the world until the present time. Nor will there ever again be anything like it. But the Lord has reduced the number of those days; if he had not, nobody would survive. For the sake of his chosen people, however, he has reduced those days' (Mark 13: 19f). With these words Jesus was apparently referring to something beyond the fall of Jerusalem, something more than a crisis within history. For to speak of distress such as will never happen again is surely to speak of the *final* crisis of history, before the End comes. But severe though that crisis may be, God will curtail it out of love for his people.

We saw at the beginning of this chapter how Jesus' disciples in their question mingled together historical events and the Final Event. They mingled together the fall of Jerusalem and the end of this age. And we see how Jesus mingled them together in his reply. Why? Because they *are* related. In the crises of history the final crisis is foreshadowed. God's judgments in history are, so to speak, rehearsals for the final judgment. The successive embodiments of antichrist foreshadow the final outburst of the devil's rebellion before the End. So Jesus was telling us that the events of A.D. 70 were a prelude to the ultimate show-down between God and the forces of evil.

Conflict with evil

Behind all these signs is Jesus' vivid awareness of the battle between good and evil, between God and Satan. The prophecy of world mission and the promise of the Holy Spirit to a persecuted church are marks of the triumph of God. Yet the warnings about wars, famines, false religion and judgment on Jerusalem don't suggest that evil is on the decrease. But surely both pictures are true. The twen-

tieth century has witnessed *both* a great advance of the
Christian mission in Africa, Asia and South America, *and*
the slipping back of Christian people into paganism. We
have seen *both* the destructive horror of global warfare,
and unprecedented attempts to help the poor and deprived
nations of earth.

How are we to understand the problem of evil? We are
unlikely to help the cause of Christ or of truth by regard-
ing evil as just an unfortunate quirk in human nature.
The New Testament has much to say about 'principalities
and powers' – forces of spiritual darkness doing battle with
the advancing reign of God. If you dismiss these powers
as mere mythology, how else do you explain, not only
plain human wickedness like stealing and murder, but also
the appalling perversion of human goodness? After all, it
is the God-given creativity of decent, law-abiding men
which enables them to invent the machines of modern
warfare. It was the God-given brain of a research scientist in America which hit on the idea of adding an extra
chemical to napalm, so that the 'new, improved' product
would cling more tenaciously to its victim to do its dis-
figuring work. It is a prosperous, civilized society which
lets an old man lie for weeks on the floor of his flat in
Nottingham, dead and undiscovered because no one cared
about him.

But we saw in chapter two how the coming of Jesus
meant victory over evil. His exorcisms demonstrated it,
his cross achieved it. Why then this continuing conflict?
Why are the forces of evil so very much alive? Because
although Christ won the victory *in principle* at his first
coming, the victory will not be *complete* until his return.
Look at it like this.

In the second world war, after Stalingrad and El
Alamein the General Staffs of both the Allied and the
German armies knew that the decisive battles had already
taken place. The result was already decided. Yet still to
come was the German use of the V–2 rockets, the mass
extermination of the Jews, bloody conflict with the resis-

tance movement. Civilians in occupied countries could be forgiven for suspecting that the enemy had the upper hand. Even as late as the winter of 1945 the Germans managed to carry off tactical manoeuvres which looked very much like victories. The outcome of the war was known to the German generals as early as 1943, but Hitler refused to admit it and the war went on until a final submission was achieved.

In a similar way, Paul could write in one letter, 'On that cross Christ freed himself from the power of the spiritual rulers and authorities; he made a public spectacle of them by leading them as captives in his victory procession' (Colossians 2: 15). Yet elsewhere he wrote, 'Christ *will* overcome all spiritual rulers, authorities and powers. . . . For Christ must rule until God defeats all enemies and puts them under his feet' (1 Corinthians 15: 24f). In principle the triumph is achieved, but the mopping-up operations are still in progress.

Evil does its work in people. And the New Testament writers allude to a figure known as 'antichrist' who embodies evil in human form. The First Letter of John declares: 'My children, it is the last hour! You have heard that antichrist is coming. Now many antichrists have appeared, and so we know that it is the last hour' (1 John 2: 18). Who are these antichrists? People who deny that Jesus really was God in human flesh (1 John 2: 22; 4: 3).

In a strange and difficult passage Paul refers to the same idea with his term 'the man of wickedness' (2 Thessalonians 2). This figure will come as the agent of Satan, will claim for himself the worship and the powers which rightly belong only to God, and will dominate men until Christ appears in glory at his coming. The book of Revelation expresses the same concept in its description of the 'beast' (Revelation 13).

Who is this antichrist? King James I thought he was the pope. More recently he has been identified with Hitler, Stalin, Mao Tse-Tung and other dictators. Certainly in our own day the kind of embodiment of evil described by Paul

and John seems to be more and more of a possibility. His-
torian Arnold Toynbee writes: 'By making more and more
lethal weapons, and at the same time making the world
more and more interdependent economically, technology
has brought mankind to such a degree of distress that we
are ripe for the deifying of any Caesar who might succeed
in giving the world unity and peace.'

Since rash suggestions about the identity of the antichrist have been made throughout history, we would be
wise not to make too hasty conclusions about who he is.
And when we remember that John's First Letter speaks
of 'many antichrists' active in his own day, we can see that
every notable embodiment of evil, *every* self-styled rival
to Jesus Christ, is in a sense antichrist. And we shall be
on our guard against them all. But we shall not be surprised if a still more terrifying and blasphemous 'man of
wickedness' is yet to appear as a prelude to the coming
of Christ.

Be on your guard!

Finally, let's recall why Jesus gave us these signs. It was
not so that we could work out a timetable of events leading up to his final coming. Jesus himself ruled that idea out
completely: 'No one knows when that day or hour will
come – neither the angels in heaven, nor the Son; only
the Father knows' (Mark 13: 32). And he told his disciples
there would be no 'early warning system' to indicate that
his coming was just around the corner. 'The time will
come', he said, 'when you will wish you could see one of
the days of the Son of Man' (this unique phrase probably
means the time immediately preceding Christ's coming).
'But you will not see it. There will be those who will say,
"Look, over there! " or "Look, over here! " But don't go
out looking for it. As the lightning flashes across the sky
and lights it up from one side to the other, so will the Son
of Man be in his day' (Luke 17: 22–24).

No, Jesus gave the signs to warn his followers about the

troubles and challenges that lay ahead of them. He knew the pressures that might destroy their faith. He knew that sufferings might seem too hard to bear. He knew the challenge to evangelize the world might seem too daunting. He knew that false teaching could reduce the Church from a powerful army to a toothless debating society. So he warned: 'Keep awake, be on your guard!' And he promised: 'The person who holds out to the end will be saved.' And from the time of Peter, Andrew, James and John to the present day and beyond, his words have been there to be acted on.

For further reading

*C. E. Armerding and W. W. Gasque (eds.), *Handbook of Biblical Prophecy* (Baker, 1977)

M. Bordeaux, *Faith on Trial in Russia* (Hodder, 1971)

Questions for Discussion

1. What kinds of things may lead us astray from Jesus as we look forward to his second coming? How can we resist these dangers?
2. Why are people continually trying to predict the date of Jesus' return?
3. 'Be on watch, be alert, for you do not know when the time will be' (Mark 13:33). How, in practical terms, do we do this?
4. Study Ephesians 6:10–20. How does Paul describe the 'opposition' which the Christian faces? What is the 'armour' provided by God, and how are we to use it?

4

THE COMING OF CHRIST

When the 'signs' reach their climax, 'then the Son of Man will appear, coming in the clouds with great power and glory' (Mark 13: 26). It is at this point that some Christians overflow with confidence, as though they know every detail about the future, while others overflow only with doubts and misgivings. Let's look first at the doubts. Why do we find it hard to believe what the Bible states and what our ancestors confidently proclaimed?

The scientific revolution

It was disturbing enough when Copernicus discovered, nearly five hundred years ago, that the earth isn't the centre of the universe. It was even more upsetting when astronomers discovered that the sun isn't the centre either – the universe is apparently boundless, it has no centre! When you're faced with this situation, how can you have the audacity to believe that some divine figure will come in clouds of glory and bring to an end our insignificant little world? Actually, it seems to me no more or less difficult to believe that, than to believe that our planet was ever visited by God in the first place. If you reject the idea of Christ's return, you must logically deny also that Jesus of Nazareth was God in human flesh.

But scientific discoveries raise another problem. We now have some idea how long the earth has been in existence. If you were to represent the whole period from the earth's beginnings to the present day by a line a hundred yards long, only the last inch or two of the line would represent the time during which man has dwelt on the earth. And many scientists estimate that – barring nuclear war or collision with another heavenly body – the earth is capable of continuing for millions more years before becoming so cold that it can't support life. So can we imagine that God will bring the world to an end in a public way, as traditionally envisaged in the Christian view of the Last Things? The vastness of these facts fill us with wonder, but it can so easily be the wonder of perplexity rather than wonder at the greatness of God the Creator.

Three things may be said about this. First, it was after all 'insignificant man' who *discovered* that the universe is bigger and longer-lived than he previously thought. So although man and his earth have been ousted from the centre of the universe, by this very understanding of this fact man has placed himself once again at the centre. And although man is a late arrival in the history of our planet, his ability to understand this enhances his position as the crown of God's creation. His significance is undiminished, his place in God's purposes unchanged.

Secondly, if the history of man and the world is *not* to be brought to a climax by the coming of Christ, what alternative possibilities are there? Is God the Creator and Sustainer of the universe or not? If he is, what is so unreasonable about the idea that he will act to transform it at some future time?

And thirdly, we would be wise not to make our faith too subject to the findings of science. Science and faith are not opposed to each other. They are answering different sets of questions. For example, when questions are asked about the creation of the universe, the scientist may suggest *how* the world came to be as it is, while the book of Genesis is concerned about the religious questions of *who* made the world and what was his *purpose* in doing so. Similarly, the scientist may tell us what the possibilities are for the continued existence of the universe. But the Bible is concerned about *who* ultimately controls the future of the universe and what *purpose* he is seeking to fulfil. What's more, the living God is constantly springing surprises on us, doing things that were beyond our power to imagine.

In the realm of technology, for instance, achievements once declared impossible by responsible people are now everyday events. On the very day that the Wright brothers flew the first aeroplane, newspapers refused to report the event because their sober editors couldn't bring themselves to believe that it had happened. After all, a famous American astronomer, Simon Newcomb, had not long before assured the world that 'no possible combination of known substances, known forms of machinery and known forms of force, can be united in a practical machine by which man shall fly long distances'.

In the realm of nature, if caterpillars could think as we do, they would be surprised to find themselves transformed into butterflies and able to enjoy a whole new mode of living. Tadpoles would disbelieve us if we told them that one day they would be set free from the limitations of wriggling round a pond.

And in the spiritual realm, who would have dreamt that in a smelly stable at the back of a pub in a despised province of the Roman empire God would choose to enter human life? Who would have dreamt in the early eighteenth century that the Evangelical Revival was about to transform the face of England? After all, in 1722 Daniel Defoe had summed up the situation when he wrote: 'No age since the founding and forming of the Christian Church, was ever like, in open avowed atheism, blasphemies, and heresies, to the age we now live in'. This is the kind of creative, onward-moving God we believe in, and he is not at the mercy of our scientific theories.

Lack of evidence

A second reason why Christian hope is out of favour is lack of evidence. If the hope of Christ's return rests merely on the word of a man 1900 years ago, how can Christians be so certain about it? How can we tell that it isn't just wishful thinking? Might it not be a case of our believing that Christ will return to sort everything out because we *want* to believe it, because we couldn't bear to live if it weren't true?

To this question the New Testament replies like this. No, it isn't wish-fulfilment, because if you are a Christian you already know the One who is to come. The Jesus whom you worship came to bring in a new age, and his coming makes no sense unless what he began is to be brought to fulfilment. Already you experience the power of the Holy Spirit in your life. And the Holy Spirit is a foretaste – only a foretaste, but a real taste – of the life which you will experience in the presence of Christ after his final coming. That is what Paul means when he says God 'gave the Holy Spirit in our hearts as the *guarantee* of all that he has for us' (2 Corinthians 1: 22). God does not mock you. He has shown himself to be full of love and utterly faithful, and he will bring to fulfilment what he has already begun. It is because we are already 'citizens of heaven' that we can confidently and 'eagerly wait for our Saviour to come from heaven, the Lord Jesus Christ' (Philippians 3: 20).

Something else which pushes Christ's return into the background is *a proper concern with the present*. We seem to have enough on our hands trying to cope with present problems. '*Now* is what matters', and to speak of future pipe-dreams seems irrelevant. This is an understandable but short-sighted viewpoint. The truth is that our achievements in the present are influenced by our ultimate goals, as I shall try to show in chapter ten. That is why people with the keenest anticipation of the Last Things have often dealt most energetically with current problems. There was, for instance, Lord Shaftesbury who did so much to stop exploitation of child labour in the early nineteenth century. Towards the end of his life he said, 'I do not think that in the last forty years I have lived one conscious hour that was not influenced by the thought of our Lord's return'. People who try to improve the present situation without any ultimate purpose in view can easily become like brilliant footballers, dribbling their way round every obstacle on the field, but achieving little because there are no goalposts at the other end.

The problem of delay

Here is a further difficulty. The longer the delay of Christ's return, the more remote the possibility becomes. Already in the Second Letter of Peter we find the warning that scoffers will say, 'He promised to come, didn't he? Where is he? Our fathers have already died, but everything is still the same as it was since the creation of the world!' The reply is not so glib as it sounds: 'There is no difference in the Lord's sight between one day and a thousand years: to him the two are the same' (2 Peter 3: 4–9). In other words, God's time-scale is bigger than ours, and in any case the date doesn't matter. The important thing is not that Christ's return is near, but that it is *intended* – by a God whose faithfulness is well-known.

But this leads us to a final reason why for many people Christ's return is a subject for doubt rather than confidence: *fanaticism has discredited the doctrine.* In particular, history is strewn with records of people who have tried to calculate the date – despite Jesus' declaration that the date of his return was unknown except to God. They have always been wrong. There was, for example, the nineteenth century Roman Catholic priest who wrote a book predicting that the world would end in 1847. On seeking the church's permission to publish the book, he was granted permission to publish it in 1848. Far from making the doctrine of Christ's return vivid and relevant, this unholy lust for certainty has made many people sceptical about the whole idea. And who can blame them? But we must distinguish between true biblical teaching and these unbiblical additions to it.

I shall say more about 'date-fixing' in chapter seven.

But let us now turn to what Jesus and his apostles *do* say about his second coming.

The manner of his coming

First, let's clear away a small difficulty. Sometimes people object to the term 'second coming' on the grounds that it is not biblical. It is true that the exact term appears nowhere in the Bible. But the writer to the Hebrews comes very close to it: 'Christ was offered in sacrifice once to take away the sins of many. He will appear *a second time*, not to deal with sin, but to save those who are waiting for him' (Hebrews 9: 28). So the term 'second coming' does sum up the New Testament emphasis on a future, final coming of Christ. Of course, we must not assume from this that between his first and second comings Christ is *absent* from the world and the Church. Far from it. Jesus' final words in Matthew's Gospel are: 'Remember! I will be with you always, to the end of the age' (Matthew 28: 20). And that, as David Livingstone said, is the promise of a perfect gentleman, who never breaks his word. Through his Spirit, Christ is continually present and active in his world. So when we speak of his second coming we are not suggesting that he has been absent since his resurrection and ascension. We are saying that whereas Christ's presence now is spiritual and invisible, his presence then will be public and visible, and he will bring this age to a close. So here are four truths about the manner of Jesus' coming.

First, it will occur at *an unexpected time*. Jesus couldn't have made this any plainer than he did: 'No one knows when that day and hour will come – neither the angels in heaven, nor the Son; the Father alone knows' (Mark 13: 32). But Luke adds some extra details:

'As it was in the time of Noah, so shall it be in the days of the Son of Man. Everybody kept on eating and drinking, men and women married, up to the very day Noah went into the ark and the Flood came and killed them all.

It will be as it was in the time of Lot. Everybody kept on eating and drinking, buying and selling, planting and building. On the day Lot left Sodom, fire and sulphur rained down from heaven and killed them all. That is how it will be on the day the Son of Man is revealed' (Luke 17: 26–30).

Well, what's so wrong with eating and drinking, getting married and building houses? Nothing. That's just the point. Just as when God sent judgment in the past, Christ will come when men and women are going about their normal everyday business, without thought of God. There will be millions of ordinary people guilty of no great crime – except that they gave no thought to the most important thing in life.

But Jesus' followers, too, may be caught by surprise. We don't know the date of his coming, but ignorance is no excuse for being unprepared. It's a reason for constant watchfulness. Jesus told a parable to illustrate this. 'It will be like a man who goes away from home on a trip and leaves his servants in charge, each one with his own work to do; and he tells the doorkeeper to keep watch. Watch, then, because you do not know when the master of the house is coming' (Mark 13: 34f).

The story is often told of the nineteenth century Scottish pastor Robert Murray M'Cheyne, who once asked some friends, 'Do you think that Christ will come tonight?' One after another they replied, 'I think not'. When they had all given the same answer, M'Cheyne solemnly repeated the text, 'In such an hour as ye think not the Son of Man cometh' (Matthew 24: 44). So date-setting is impossible, and Christ demands nothing less than constant readiness. What form this readiness should take we shall see in later chapters.

A second point about Jesus' coming is that it is *always near*, as he showed in another parable in Mark 13: 'Let the fig tree teach you a lesson. When its branches become green and tender, and it starts putting out leaves, you know that summer is near. In the same way, when you see these things happening (that is, the signs listed earlier in Mark

13), you will know that the time (of my return) is near, ready to begin. Remember this! All these things (the signs) will happen before the people now living have all died' (Mark 13: 28–30).

This leads us into another difficulty. If these signs were to appear during the lifetime of Jesus' hearers – and they did – what has happened to Jesus' promise that they showed the nearness of his return? Was he mistaken? And if he said his coming was near, doesn't that contradict his claim that he didn't know the time of his coming? The truth is that the events of Jesus' incarnation, crucifixion, resurrection, ascension and second coming are in a real sense parts of *one act of God*. They are all part of the coming of God's kingly rule, and the climax is only delayed by the mercy of God who desires to give men opportunity to respond to the gospel. Therefore in a real sense the second coming is always near ever since Jesus began the new era through his life, death and resurrection. I know this is not easy for us to grasp, but I believe it is the best way to understand the apparent contradictions in Jesus' own teaching.

A saying of Jesus which offers a similar problem and invites the same solution is Mark 9: 1: 'There are some here who will not die until they have seen the kingdom of God come with power'. In a sense the kingdom of God *was* near. Its power *was* made known before Jesus' disciples had all died – in the events of Pentecost, the judgment on Jerusalem, the rapid movement of the gospel throughout the Roman empire. Yet it did not come in a final way – the climax still lay in some unknown future time. But 'unknown' could mean 'soon'.

Thirdly, Christ's coming will be *a public event*. In complete contrast to his coming at Bethlehem, there will be nothing hidden or obscure about his return. 'The Son of Man will come like the lightning which flashes across the whole sky from east to west' (Matthew 24: 27). And Jesus used even more vivid language than that: 'In the days after that time of trouble the sun will grow dark, the moon will no longer shine, the stars will fall from heaven, and the powers in space will be driven from their course. Then the Son of Man will appear, coming in the clouds with great power and glory' (Mark 13: 24–26). This is dramatic picture-language taken from the Old Testament. After all, if we are trying to speak of something which is beyond our present experience and bigger than anything we can understand, we can only do it in language which goes beyond what is normal. Some people I know even get carried away when trying to describe their girl-friends or boy-friends. How much more is this to be expected when you're looking for words to describe the climax of history? Whatever the details may mean, Jesus was surely pointing to the public nature of his final coming.

Fourthly, he will come *in triumph*. His first coming was in humiliation and suffering, to be despised and rejected by men. Not so his future coming. His reference to clouds, power and glory show that he will come in triumph, with the full authority of God behind him. Through his suffering he conquered the power of evil. At his coming he will claim that victory, so that 'all will openly proclaim that Jesus Christ is the Lord, to the glory of God the Father' (Philippians 2: 11).

The purpose of his coming

The Bible pays more attention to the question, *Why* will Jesus come?, than to the question, *How* will he come? And so should we. The two main purposes – resurrection and judgment – will be looked at in the next two chapters. Here we may mention four others.

First, *God will complete the plan he began in Christ*. The reign of God which Jesus brought among men will be finally and totally established. There will be an end of suffering, death and temptation to evil.

Second, *God will bring history to a climax*. Despite appearances, history is not a meaningless succession of events, 'a tale told by an idiot, full of sound and fury, signifying nothing'. Of course, you can't *prove* that history is moving towards a goal, any more than you can *prove* that God was acting in Israel's escape from Egypt under Moses, or in the invasion of Israel by the Assyrians, or indeed in the coming of Jesus himself. It's a matter of faith, not sight. But the biblical faith is that when you look at history in the light of its End, you can see that all the chaotic movements of history, all the ups and downs, fall into place as part of the onward movement of God's purposes. It's as if you were to read the last chapter of a detective thriller to find out how it all turns out, and *then* read the story from the beginning, picking up as you go along the clues you would have missed if you hadn't read the last chapter first. And so the day is coming when history will reach its goal and give way to God's eternity.

Thirdly, the hope of Christ's return emphasizes that *to establish the kingdom is God's act.* The kingdom of God is not something which we 'spread' or 'build' – the nature of èvil is too serious for that to be possible. The coming of God's kingdom is God's act. Prophets, apostles and Jesus himself all agreed that the perfect kingdom of God could only become a reality by a supernatural, world-transforming act of God. So we long for Christ's return to bring this about.

The final, joyful fact is that this coming will be *the coming of Christ.* When we come to history's end we shall not face a distant, unknown figure. God has already shown us what kind of a Person it is with whom we shall have to do. We shall encounter the same Person whose holiness, truth and utter love we already know in Christ. The end of the world is no mere event, but a meeting with a Person – the Person whose suffering love has brought God's reign near to us. That is why in Revelation 5, the Lion of the tribe of Judah who comes in triumph is also the Lamb who was killed and bears the marks of slaughter upon him. Written on the pages of history from beginning to end is love – personal, self-giving love. And it is that Love which will meet us on the final day.

For further reading

B. Milne, *The End of the World* (Kingsway Bible Teaching Series, Kingsway, 1979)
*I. Murray, *The Puritan Hope* (Banner of Truth, 1971)
*S. H. Travis, *Christian Hope and the Future of Man* (IVP, 1980)

Questions for Discussion

1. How prominent is the theme of the return of Christ in your own thinking and in your church? If it isn't prominent, should anything be done about it?
2. What difference does a belief in the second coming make to the Christian life? Why is it not enough merely to have the fact of Jesus' presence with us now?
3. If 'to establish the kingdom is God's act', is there anything we can do to bring it nearer?
4. Study 1 Thessalonians 4: 13–5: 11. What assurances does Paul give about Christians who have died? What warnings does he give about the time of Christ's return? What instructions for Christian living does he give in the light of Jesus' return?

5

THE GREAT DIVIDE

No theme is so prominent in the Bible and so neglected by Christians today as the theme of judgment. Throughout the New Testament we are told that Jesus' coming will be followed by judgment. There is a dramatic passage, full of Jewish imagery, in Paul's Second Letter to the church at Thessalonica:

'God will do what is right: he will bring suffering on those who make you suffer, and he will give relief to you who suffer, and to us as well. He will do this when the Lord Jesus appears from heaven with his mighty angels, with a flaming fire, to punish those who do not know God and those who do not obey the Good News about our Lord Jesus. They will suffer the punishment of eternal destruction, separated from the presence of the Lord and from his glorious might, when he comes on that Day to receive glory from all his people and honour from all who believe' (2 Thessalonians 1: 6–10).

But no one spoke of judgment more often or more clearly than Jesus himself. 'When the Son of Man comes as King, and all the angels with him, he will sit on his royal throne, and all the earth's people will be gathered before him. Then he will divide them into two groups, just as a shepherd separates the sheep from the goats: he will put the sheep at his right hand and the goats at his left . . .' (Matthew 25: 31–33).

An unpopular idea

It doesn't take a genius to point out that Jesus' warnings of judgment are not very welcome. After all, we like to run our own lives. And to be told that there is a Judge, Someone standing over us, reminds us that we are both finite and guilty – and we don't like it. Bishop John Robinson has observed: 'We live, in this twentieth century, in a world without judgment, a world where at the last frontier post you simply go out – and nothing happens. It is like coming to the customs and finding there are none after all. And the suspicion that this is in fact the case spreads fast: for it is what we should all like to believe' [*On Being the Church in the World*, 1969, p. 165].

Christian preachers haven't always helped, either. Sometimes lacking in love, they have given the impression of believing what this old verse expresses:

'We are the chosen few,
All others will be damned;
There is no room in heaven for you,
We can't have heaven crammed.'

So the idea has got around that Christians believe in a God who cheerfully exults in declaring with the Mikado,

'My object all sublime
I shall achieve in time,
To let the punishment fit the crime'.

How different from the Father of Jesus! God's wrath, says James Stewart, is his love in agony, 'smitten with dreadful sorrow'.

We dare not neglect it

Judgment is an unpopular subject, but what happens if we ignore it? Many people think that if you remove the idea of judgment you set men free from fears and taboos. Far from it. What you do is make men *less* than men. For example, if you excuse a criminal from punishment you are making him less than man because you are denying his responsibility for his action, and responsibility is an essential part of human personality. In the same way, if you deny that all of us are responsible *for* our actions and responsible *to* God, you are denying an essential part of human personality and reducing us to the level of machines.

I am not, of course, suggesting that a court ought never to make allowances for an offender's background and circumstances when it passes sentence. Nor am I denying that when God judges us he takes into account what opportunities we have had to respond to his love – 'As for you, Capernaum . . . , if the miracles which were performed in you had been performed in Sodom, it would still be in existence today! Remember, then, that on the Judgment Day God will show more mercy to Sodom than to you! ' (Matthew 11: 23f). But if you deny altogether that men are responsible to God, you take away one of the most precious things about their humanity.

Also, consider Jesus' words: 'On the Judgment Day everyone will have to give account of every useless word he has ever spoken' (Matthew 12: 36). This isn't something merely to be feared, but to be welcomed, because it means that God sees all our actions as important. If you remove the idea of judgment, then in the long run *no* actions are important.

In the world today, with our pollution of the earth and our rape of its resources, we are experiencing the results of men's refusal to believe that God will judge them. We destroy the earth because we think we can get away with it. Only when men come to believe that all life is held in trust from God will we have an adequate reason why we owe a duty to posterity and why we should treat the earth and all its creatures responsibly. Bishop Hugh Montefiore has boldly declared: 'Belief in man's creatureliness and in his accountability before God seem literally essential for the future salvation of this planet' [*Can Man Survive?*, 1970, p. 56].

Who will be our Judge on the Day of Judgment? Someone has expressed it like this:

'The Long Silence'

'At the end of time, billions of people were scattered on a great plain before God's throne.

Most shrank back from the brilliant light before them. But some groups near the front talked heatedly – not with cringing shame, but with belligerence.

"Can God judge us? How can he know about suffering?" snapped a pert young brunette. She ripped open a sleeve to reveal a tattooed number from a Nazi concentration camp.
"We endured terror . . . beatings . . . torture . . . death!"

In another group a Negro boy lowered his collar.
"What about this?" he demanded, showing an ugly rope burn.
"Lynched for no crime but being black!"

In another crowd, a pregnant schoolgirl with sullen eyes. "Why should I suffer?" she murmured. "It wasn't my fault."

Far out across the plain were hundreds of such groups. Each had a complaint against God for the evil and suffering he permitted in his world.

How lucky God was to live in heaven where all was sweetness and light, where there was no weeping or fear, no hunger or hatred.

What did God know of all that men had been forced to endure in this world? For God leads a pretty sheltered life, they said.

So each of these groups sent forth their leader, chosen because he had suffered the most. A Jew, a Negro, a person from Hiroshima, a horribly deformed arthritic, a thalidomide child.

In the centre of the plain they consulted with each other. At last they were ready to present their case. It was rather clever.

Before God could be qualified to be their judge, he must endure what they had endured. Their decision was that God should be sentenced to live on earth – as a man!

Let him be born a Jew. Let the legitimacy of his birth be doubted.

Give him a work so difficult that even his family will think him out of his mind when he tries to do it. Let him be betrayed by his closest friends. Let him face false charges, be tried by a prejudiced jury and convicted by a cowardly judge. Let him be tortured.

At the last, let him see what it means to be terribly alone. Then let him die. Let him die so that there can be no doubt he died.

Let there be a great host of witnesses to verify it.

As each leader announced his portion of the sentence, loud murmurs of approval went up from the throng of people assembled.

When the last had finished pronouncing sentence there was a long silence.

No one uttered another word. No one moved.

For suddenly all knew that

God had already served his sentence.'

Jesus will be our Judge. 'God has given him the right to judge, because he is the Son of Man. Do not be surprised at this; for the time is coming when all the dead in the graves will hear his voice, and they will come out of their graves : Those who have done good will be raised and live, and those who have done evil will be raised and be condemned' (John 5: 27–29). When the author of Revelation uses that startling phrase 'the wrath of the Lamb' (Revelation 6: 16), he is picturing the Judge not as a powerful or destructive animal, but as the Lamb who offered himself up for our salvation and whose sacrificial love men are constantly rejecting.

The choice is yours

By our attitude to Christ, by the choices we make, our destinies are being decided now. In that sense judgment is already at work. 'This is how judgment works: the light has come into the world, but men love the darkness rather than the light, because they do evil things. And anyone who does evil things hates the light and will not come to the light, because he does not want his evil deeds to be shown up' (John 3: 19f). By the choices they make, men sentence themselves.

And the process goes on. Imagine a man, says Leon Morris, who is determined to build up his business and make money, even though it involves him in shady practices and necessitates that bowing down to mammon which is incompatible with Christ. 'He builds up his business, he makes his money. Never let it be said that God in harsh revenge for the man's success has shut him out of heaven. He has shut himself out. He set on his immortal soul the price of his business. And he proceeded to sell himself for that' [*The Biblical Doctrine of Judgment*, 1960, p. 52].

The choice is ours. If in the end we find ourselves outside the kingdom of God, it will be because we have refused to enter the kingdom now. Jesus urgently appealed to men to enter God's kingdom while there is still time. In his parables there is the landowner going repeatedly to the market-place and inviting the men who are outside his vineyard to come and work for him (Matthew 20: 1–16). There is the tragedy of the guests's pathetic refusal to come to the wedding of the king's son, and the king's urgent invitation to others to come and take their place (Matthew 22: 1–10). And there is Jesus' plain statement: 'Whoever does not receive the kingdom of God like a child shall never enter it' (Mark 10: 15).

When Christ comes and the final judgment takes place, he will underline the choices we have made. Precisely how it will all take place is not important. But the dramatic biblical picture of the Great Assize with Christ sitting on his judgment-throne captures several important truths: judgment is serious, it is just, it is inescapable. And it is judgment under the searching gaze of holy love – judgment by Christ himself. As Studdert Kennedy expresses it:

> 'There ain't no throne, and there ain't no books,
> It's 'Im you've got to see.'

The final judgment

What will judgment mean on that day? Let's notice three truths about it.

First, *all men will be judged.* 'When the Son of Man comes as king, . . . all the earth's people will be gathered before him' for judgment (Matthew 25: 31). That was Jesus' message. And Peter later announced that 'he commanded us to preach the gospel to the people, and to testify that he is the one whom God has appointed Judge of the living and the dead' (Acts 10: 42).

None will escape, and religious people are no more exempt from this examination than anyone else. Jesus said it is possible to perform religious acts and still be a stranger to him – 'When that day comes, many will say to me, "Lord, Lord! In your name we told God's message, by your name we drove out many demons and performed many miracles!" Then I will say to them, "I never knew you. Away from me, you evildoers!" ' (Matthew 7: 22f).

This message of the last judgment is not intended to undermine our assurance, but to remove complacency, that besetting sin of religious people. Salvation does not lie in buildings or traditions or even in religious experiences, but in Christ himself. The purpose of the judgment will be to reveal who is a true follower of Christ.

Secondly, *we shall be judged according to our deeds.* 'The Son of Man is to come in the glory of his Father with his angels', said Jesus, 'and then he will repay everyone according to his deeds' (Matthew 16: 27). And the other

New Testament writers agree – much to the embarrass-
ment of many Christians, who sense a conflict with the
doctrine of justification through faith. How can both these
doctrines be correct? How are we to reconcile them? The
answer is, as C. H. Spurgeon said in another context, 'I
never reconcile friends'. They are two complementary
truths, and the problem only arises when justification is
misunderstood.

'To be 'justified' means to be brought into a right relationship with God, so that you experience God's power at
work in your life. But, like any gift, it is only yours if you
receive it and make use of it. So justification through faith,
though it is a gift of God's sheer grace, lays upon us the
responsibility to work out our new status in practice. The
only kind of faith in which God is interested is faith which
shows its reality by the deeds it produces. 'What matters
is faith that works through love' (Galatians 5: 6). And at
the final judgment a man's deeds will be the evidence of
the kind of man he is. It's not a question of our earning
salvation by good works: works are the evidence that our
faith is real.

When Jesus spoke of the final judgment, he said the
outcome would depend on what we have done for the
poor, the imprisoned, the hungry, the friendless immigrant
(Matthew 25: 31–46). Jesus, the suffering Son of Man,
identifies with all who suffer and are in need and says:
'You show what your attitude to me is by the way you
react to your fellow-men in their suffering. And on that
reaction depends your eternal destiny.'

So faith and works go very closely together. If you
believe in the real, biblical Christ – one who cares for the
suffering, cares about men's physical as well as spiritual
needs, is concerned about justice – then your belief must
have a wide range of practical effects. The trouble is that
what we believe is often watered down to make it less
demanding.

At the final judgment, it will not just be our outward
deeds that come under examination. There are many who

have never been found guilty of any crime by a human law-court, and yet inwardly are seething with bitterness, hatred or sheer self-centred smugness. All this will be revealed 'on that Day when God, through Jesus Christ, will judge all the secret thoughts of men' (Romans 2: 16). Our deeds, our words, our thoughts, our motives, our characters will all be laid bare before God. 'Every one of us will have to give account of *himself* to God' (Romans 14: 12). All the information will be available, and there will be no miscarriage of justice. If allowances have to be made for some people's background or limited opportunities to respond to Christ, we may trust the loving and all knowing God to deal justly with those situations.

We aren't responsible for our background or our natural gifts. But we *are* responsible for our character, and the direction in which we set it determines our destiny. 'Do not deceive yourselves: no one makes a fool of God. A man will reap exactly what he plants. If he plants in the field of his natural desires, from it he will gather the harvest of death; if he plants in the field of the Spirit, from the Spirit he will gather the harvest of eternal life' (Galatians 6: 7f).

The third point is this. *Judgment means division.* Dr Samuel Johnson remarked: 'I remember that my Maker has said that he will place the sheep on his right hand, and the goats on his left. That is a solemn truth which this frivolous age needs to hear, for it strikes at the very roots of life and destiny.' His 'frivolous age' was the eighteenth century, but frivolity hasn't entirely died out.

Jesus said that when he comes again 'he will send out the angels to the four corners of the earth and gather God's chosen people from one end of the world to the other' (Mark 13: 27). Surely this implies a separation between those who belong to 'God's chosen people' and those who do not? Elsewhere the division is made explicit. 'At that time two men will be working in the field: one will be taken away, the other will be left behind.' (Matthew 24: 40f).

Men divide themselves now by choice into believers and unbelievers. They need not suppose it will be any different at the final judgment, when God underlines the choices we have made. If we have fellowship with God now, we shall enter into a fuller experience of his presence then. If we do not know him now, we shall not know him then. Those who are unprepared for that day will be like the foolish girls whose oil-lamps ran out when they were waiting for the wedding to begin. While they went off to buy some more oil, the bridegroom arrived, the celebrations began, and when they got back they found the door closed. They were too late to get in (Matthew 25: 1–12).

It will be no use protesting that God ought to have given us a 'second chance 'after death. God is *continually* offering us chances to respond to his love. C. S. Lewis declares somewhere that we must grow out of a fairy-tale attitude which says everything will turn out all right in the end. We live in a *real* world with *real* choices to be made. And the way that we choose affects our lives now and in the future.

God has given us the amazing privilege of freedom to choose. That is what makes us human. And having given us freedom God won't take it away by dragging unwilling rebels into heaven. God's love will not overrule our freedom. Love can never force, or it would cease to be love. God can't take us by the scruff of the neck and say, 'You *will* believe' – if he did that he would not be loving us. *Because* God loves us, he will not interfere with our freedom. And if we insist on rejecting him he will let us – like the father who allows the prodigal son to run off on his own and make a mess of his life, even though he longs for his son to come home. It is God's respect for human freedom that makes hell possible.

When the Great Divide takes place, those who belong to Christ will be welcomed into his presence. Those who have turned their backs on his love, pooh-poohed his forgiveness and rejected his way of life will have their choice underlined. Is it surprising that John in his vision sees them wanting to hide from the majesty of Christ when they find themselves exposed? 'They called out to the mountains and to the rocks. "Fall down on us and hide us from the eyes of the one who sits upon the throne, and from the wrath of the Lamb! For the great day of their wrath is here, and who can stand up against it?"' (Revelation 6: 16f).

The day of judgment will mean the welcome of God's people into his presence. It will mark the end of all resistance to his will. But above all it is the day when Jesus Christ himself will be at the centre of the scene, when he comes 'to receive glory from all his people and honour from all who believe' (2 Thessalonians 1: 10).

Until then God's offer of a new beginning is still open. If Christ's coming is delayed, it is because 'he is patient with you, because he does not want anyone to be destroyed, but wants all to turn away from their sins' (2 Peter 3: 9). If men persist in turning down an offer like that, who is to blame for the consequences? Not God.

For further reading

C. S. Lewis, *The Problem of Pain* (Fontana, 1957)

Questions for Discussion

1. Why do you think it is that while Christians are reluctant to use the word 'hell', film and novel titles are full of it?
2. 'I believe in a God of love who is too merciful to condemn anyone.' How would you reply to this objection to the idea of God's judgment?
3. A teenager who has rebelled against the Christian faith of his parents is killed in a motor-cycle accident. What would you say to his parents who are concerned about his eternal destiny?
4. Study John 3: 16–21. What does it teach about God's

judgment? Does the message of God's love in verse 16 make any sense without the note of judgment in the same verse? How would you explain the teaching of the passage to someone who finds the idea of God's judgment difficult to accept?

6

TOMORROW'S WORLD

A minister was visiting a man who was very ill. At the foot of the stairs the sick man's wife whispered apprehensively, 'Say something *hopeful* to him, won't you? – not about heaven and all that'.

The knowledge that this life will end creates anguish and often fear. But if there's no hope in heaven, where else can hope be found? Jesus declared that at his final coming he will 'gather God's chosen people from one end of the world to the other' (Mark 13: 27). *That's* why he's coming – to welcome those who love him into his Father's presence!

But this immediately raises a problem. What about those who die before Jesus comes? Do they go to be with Christ as soon as they die, or do they have to wait around in some disembodied state until the final resurrection when Jesus returns? Learned volumes have discussed this question in enormous detail, but perhaps they are rather irrelevant. For at death we pass beyond the earthly measurements of time. So to discuss how many years may pass between death and resurrection is really to miss the point. All who die in faith are firmly grasped by Christ's love, and will not be conscious of any passage of time until the moment when Christ returns – any more than we are conscious of time passing between our going to sleep at night and waking up in the morning. But when Christ comes 'those who have died believing in Christ will be raised to life first; then we who are living at the time will all be gathered up along with them in the clouds to meet the Lord in the air. And so we will always be with the Lord' (1 Thessalonians 4: 16f).

Whatever may be the precise meaning of this vivid picture, the important thing is not the timing, but the end-result – 'we will always be with the Lord'. Within one letter, to the church at Philippi, Paul says two things which appear contradictory. 'I want very much to leave this life and be with Christ' (Philippians 1: 23). *That* looks as though Paul expected to be with Christ immediately after death. But later he writes: 'We eagerly wait for our Saviour to come from heaven, the Lord Jesus Christ. He will change our weak mortal bodies and make them like his own glorious body' (Philippians 3: 20f). *That* suggests that we shall not be raised up into the new life of God's kingdom until Christ returns.

But the two statements aren't contradictory if we remember that our earthly time-reckonings are irrelevant beyond death. After Paul himself died, human history continued – 1900 years of it so far. But Paul is not conscious of the passing of all that time because he has passed beyond time. And still we await the day when time itself will be taken up into God's eternity, when Christ will come to call to himself all who love him, both the living and the dead.

So the timing doesn't matter. What *does* matter is that there is triumph over death for all who have accepted the new life that Christ offers. This message flashed across the first century world like a thunderbolt. It was a world oppressed by fear of death, to which the Christian message was supremely relevant.

The sting of death

It is no different today. Behind society's conspiracy of silence about death lurk the same fears, the same uncertainties, the same pessimism as in the first century.

There are many who affirm that beyond death there is – nothing. Bertrand Russell spoke for many when he wrote: 'There is darkness without, and when I die there

will be darkness within. There is no splendour, no vastness anywhere; only triviality for a moment, and then
nothing.' And Tom Stoppard's play *Rosencrantz and
Guildenstern Are Dead* echoes the same conviction, when
Guildenstern comments grimly on Hamlet's deliberations
about suicide: 'No, no. It's not like that. Death isn't
romantic . . . death is not anything . . . death is . . . not.
It's the absence of presence, nothing more . . . the endless
time of never coming back. . . . A gap you can't see, and
when the wind blows through it, it makes no sound.'

Many who cannot face such bleak pessimism conceal
the finality of death in euphemisms and sentimentality. We
no longer speak of coffins but of 'caskets', the mortuary
has become a 'chapel of rest', the dead are now 'the
deceased'. And then there is the combination of the senti-
mental and the macabre in the following lines which –
believe it or not – were a radio commercial in the United
States, sung to the tune 'Rock of Ages':

> 'Chambers' caskets are just fine,
> Made of sandalwood and pine.
> If your loved ones have to go
> Call Columbus 690.
> If your loved ones pass away,
> Have them pass the Chambers way.
> Chambers' customers all sing:
> "Death, o death, where is thy sting?" '

When you hear that sort of thing, you may find it quite
easy to respect the down-to-earth honesty of the man whose
philosophy is, 'Let us eat, drink and be merry, for tomorrow we die'. But the trouble with this is that tomorrow
we do die. So what then?

Fear and uncertainty about death have led thousands
to seek assurance in spiritism, claiming as it does to communicate with the dead. I am not concerned to argue
whether or not such attempts to communicate are successful. But what *is* significant is that the messages which
spiritist mediums receive from 'the dead' usually describe

the after-life in dull and uninspiring terms. They may offer some hint of *survival* after death, but who is interested in survival unless it involves transformation to a totally new level of life? Spiritist survival is certainly not the same as Christian hope.

After all, people in the first century knew all about survival after death. If Christians had arrived on the scene proclaiming survival, everyone would have groaned and carried on what they were doing. But what the Church *did* proclaim made people prick up their ears and ask for more. What was their message about? Not about survival or some theory of the immortality of the soul, but about resurrection – the raising up of our whole personality to a life of fulfilment in the presence of God. That really made people's hair stand on end. It really enabled them to cry,

'Where, O Death, is your victory?

Where, O Death, is your power to hurt?' (1 Corinthians 15: 55). And it still does. Who ever heard of a Marxist on his deathbed asking for *Das Kapital* to be read to him, or a let-us-eat-drink-and-be-merry man asking for a reading from *Playboy*? But thousands of Christians have died with words like these ringing in their ears:

'Who then can separate us from the love of Christ? Can trouble do it, or hardship, or persecution, or hunger, or poverty, or danger, or death? . . . No, in all these things we have complete victory thruogh him who loved us! For I am certain that nothing can separate us from his love: neither death nor life; neither angels nor other heavenly rules or powers; neither the present nor the future; neither the world above nor the world below – there is nothing in all creation that will ever be able to separate us from the love of God which is ours through Jesus Christ our Lord' (Romans 8: 35–39).

The ground of hope

Why such confidence? There are two reasons. First, we know something about God's love. God has shown through

Jesus how much he loves the people he has created. He has made us to know him – nothing less. He assures us of his presence and loving care. And if already we experience these things, how can we believe that God will abandon us to nothingness? The Father of Jesus Christ isn't like that.

The second reason for confidence is the resurrection of Jesus. 'The truth is', wrote Paul, 'that Christ has been raised from death, as the guarantee that those who sleep in death will also be raised' (1 Corinthians 15: 20). Our hope of resurrection doesn't depend on a philosophical argument but on the fact that death was defeated in the person of Jesus. It is God's declared purpose to raise from death all who are united to Christ, just as Christ himself was raised. Professor A. M. Hunter has written: 'We are living in a world in which, for all its sin and sadness, Christ has left one gaping tomb in earth's wide graveyard . . . His victory is like the breach in a North Sea dyke – an event of apparently small importance whose consequences are incalculable' [*The Gospel according to St Paul*, 1966, p. 113].

The resurrection of Jesus gives us a clue to something else, too. What kind of bodies shall we have in heaven? The answer is that Christ 'will change our weak mortal bodies and make them like his own glorious body' (Philippians 3: 21). The resurrected body of Jesus is the model for the resurrection of his followers. After Jesus rose from death he was no mere ghostly figure, nor was he simply a physical body returned to life. His body was transformed, suitable to life in a new and glorious environment. It was different, yet still the same Jesus. And so it shall be with us. Paul says we shall have 'spiritual bodies' (1 Corinthians 15: 44) – personalities suited to a spiritual environment. We shall be no mere shadows of our former selves, nor shall we be physical copies of our former selves. We shall be transformed for the life of heaven. As David Winter says in his book *Hereafter*, 'just as the caterpillar has to be changed into the butterfly in order to "inherit" the air, so we have to be changed in order to "inherit" heaven'.

What an encouragement this is for the old woman crippled with arthritis, the thalidomide child, the man who lost a leg in a car crash. Such tragic disabilities will one day be forgotten for ever. We shall be transformed! What an encouragement in all the sufferings, amidst all the destructive forces that may attack us in our earthly life. 'Even though our outward nature is decaying', wrote Paul, 'our inward nature is being made new day by day. And this small and temporary trouble we suffer will bring us a tremendous and eternal glory, much greater than the trouble. For we fix our attention, not on things that are seen, but on things that are unseen. What can be seen lasts only for a time; but what cannot be seen lasts for ever' (2 Corinthians 4: 16–18). As we grow old – and perhaps weary – we are approaching not merely death, but life in all its fullness.

Life in tomorrow's world

If you were moving house next month you would want to know something about the district to which you were moving. And it's perfectly natural that we should ask questions about what heaven is like. There are many questions which can't be answered, because heaven lies beyond our experience. It's no use asking *where* heaven is, because heaven is not a material place which can be located at some particular place in the universe. It is different – superior and more glorious than anything we know on earth. But the Bible does give some clues.

First, *the universe will be transformed*. The Bible does not say that the universe will be destroyed when Christ comes, but that it will be transformed into 'new heavens and a new earth' (2 Peter 3: 13). Our Christian hope is not for escape from bodily and earthly life, but for transformed bodies in a transformed environment. In Romans 8 Paul observes that in nature itself there is conflict and imperfection. 'Yet', he goes on, 'there was this hope: that creation itself would one day be set free from its slavery to decay, and share the glorious freedom of the children of God. For we know that up to the present time all of creation groans with pain like the pain of childbirth. But not just creation alone; we who have the Spirit as the first of God's gifts, we also groan within ourselves as we wait for God to make us his sons and set our whole being free' (Romans 8: 20–23).

This is hard for us to understand, but at least it is assuring us that God will not simply write off the world which he has so intricately created. And it reminds us that the after-life is not a vague, shadowy existence, but life in an environment where the most precious things on earth – such as relationships, beauty, development, communication – can continue. Indeed, C. S. Lewis in *The Great Divorce* encourages us to imagine heaven not as something remote and less real than this life. He describes a heaven where everything is more *solid*, more *real* than on earth – a healthy corrective to our short-sighted tendency to assume that what we experience now is the only solid reality.

The book of Revelation gives some more clues about the world to come. When the new heaven and new earth appear, it says, God 'will wipe away all tears from men's eyes. There will be no more death, no more grief, crying or pain. The old things have disappeared' (Revelation 21: 4).

Then at last there will be *an end of death and suffering*. When Jesus raised men from death to life, when he healed the sick and liberated men gripped by fear of evil forces, he began something which will reach its climax when he comes to usher in the new world – his triumph over death and pain and all the grief they cause. Not for ever will suffering hold the world like a cruel tyrant in its clutches.

There will be *an end of evil* too. 'Nothing that is defiled shall enter the city' of heaven (Revelation 21: 27). And the final defeat of the powers of evil is summed up in

John's declaration that 'the Devil who deceived men will be thrown into the lake of fire and sulphur', there to be 'tormented day and night, for ever and ever' (Revelation 20: 10).

And there will be *an end of all insecurity*. There are many times when we feel weak and defeated in our fight against evil. We are oppressed by doubts and all seems dark. We feel exposed and insecure. But in God's new world all the things which now threaten our security will be gone. There will be no evil, no temptation. We shall be secure. The writer to the Hebrews describes how Abraham threw away all earthly security and 'left his own country without knowing where he was going'. Why? Because he 'was waiting for the city which God has designed and built, the city with permanent foundations' (Hebrews 11: 8, 10). 'Let us be thankful, then', he adds, 'because we receive a kingdom that cannot be shaken' (Hebrews 12: 28).

Heaven is where God is

Heaven doesn't just signal the end of all kinds of evil. There are positive things to be said as well. The most central fact of all is that heaven means *being in the presence of God* and his Son Jesus Christ. 'Where I am', Jesus promised, 'you will be too' (John 14: 3). When we love someone we aren't satisfied until we are with that person, and it's no different with our love for Christ. One day faith will give way to sight. 'Now God's home is with men! He will live with them, and they shall be his people. God himself will be with them, and he will be their God' (Revelation 21: 3).

And sight will lead to worship:

'To him who sits on the throne, and to the Lamb,
Be praise and honour, glory and might,
For ever and ever! ' (Revelation 5: 13).

This is what we were created for – 'to glorify God and to enjoy him for ever'! This is what heaven is all about –

fellowship with God which fulfils our deepest needs and our highest aspirations.

But this worship will be no private contemplation of God, for in heaven *we shall be united with all God's people*. The worshippers in the book of Revelation sing to Jesus:

'You are worthy . . .
For you were killed, and by your death
You bought men for God,
From every tribe, and language, and people, and nation'
(Revelation 5: 9).

Sometimes the Bible pictures heaven as a city – a place of community. But it will be a city very different from the cities we know, with their seductive adverts and drab back-streets, their high-rise flats and homeless families. God's city will be a place of true community – a place where 'righteousness will be at home' (2 Peter 3: 13). And not only righteousness, for God's kingdom, says Paul, is a matter of 'the righteousness and peace and joy that the Holy Spirit gives' (Romans 14: 17).

So heaven, unlike earthly cities, will be a place of total justice and righteousness. It will be a place of peace – and peace in the Bible means not just the absence of war, but a relationship of real harmony between God and men. And it will be a place of joy.

Nowhere is this sense of joy brought out more strongly than in the picture of heaven as a wedding feast. Weddings on earth are not usually dull affairs, so the angel's announcement should make our minds tingle with anticipation: '*Happy* are those who have been invited to the wedding feast of the Lamb' (Revelation 19: 9). No wonder that Dante, describing how he finally arrived in Paradise and heard the heavenly choirs singing praises to the Trinity, adds: 'It seemed like the laughter of the universe'. Laughter in heaven? If to be in the presence of God and his people means fullness of joy, what could be more appropriate?

But when we share in the community of heaven, shall

we recognize each other? Most certainly. If Jesus promised, 'Many will come from the east and the west and sit down at table in the kingdom of heaven with Abraham, Isaac and Jacob' (Matthew 8: 11), he presumably meant that Abraham and the others would be recognized. Just as Jesus' followers were able to recognize him after his resurrection, so we shall know each other – that's one reason why we shall have 'spiritual bodies'. But it will be knowledge on a deeper level, with fuller love and understanding than we have ever known before.

Love, too, is one of the solid realities of heaven, 'When Christ appears', John tells us, 'we shall become like him, because we shall see him as he really is' (1 John 3: 2). To be like Christ surely means, above all else, to be full of love. And there will be plenty of scope for that. For 'there are three things that last for ever: faith, hope and love; but the greatest of these is love' (1 Corinthians 13: 13).

This may help us to answer another question – What shall we *do* in heaven? With no timetables to worry about, shan't we just get bored stiff? No, not if love is a mark of the world to come. Love means active self-giving for others, it means service and care. And there's always scope for adventure, for growth and development in love. The details are hidden from us, but of one thing we can be sure: heaven will offer no grounds for disappointment.

'What no man ever saw or heard,
What no man ever thought could happen,
Is the very thing God prepared for those who
love him' (1 Corinthians 2: 9).

Let's note one final thing about heaven: 'The greatness and the wealth of the nations will be brought into the city' (Revelation 21: 26). We cannot tell how, but it seems that all which is good and pure in human life and culture will be taken up into God's kingdom. Heaven is no world-denying Nirvana, but an eternal 'yes' to the goodness of God's creation. The God who made the earth with all its colour and variety and breathtaking grandeur, with the splendour of its art and music and creativity, will welcome into his new world everything in the old world which has value in his sight.

God's promise is that tomorrow's world will be better than all that is best in today's world, and that should be assurance enough for anyone. It was for Dietrich Bonhoeffer, the Christian pastor executed by the Nazis in 1945. 'This is the end', were his last words to his friends. 'For me, the beginning of life'.

For further reading

P. Cotterell, *Death* (Kingsway Bible Teaching Series, Kingsway, 1979)
C. S. Lewis, *The Great Divorce* (Fontana, 1972)
D. Winter, *Hereafter* (Hodder, 1972)

Questions for Discussion

1. Is it selfish to desire to 'go to heaven'?
2. A friend tells you he is afraid to die. What will you say to him?
3. Is it possible to have a real desire for heaven without being 'so heavenly-minded that you're no earthly use'? How?
4. Study 1 Corinthians 15: 35–58. How does Paul answer the question he asks in verse 35?

7

THE CRYSTAL-BALL POLISHERS

By this time some readers are no doubt puzzled by certain omissions from this book. Why is so little said about the Old Testament promises? Why has nothing been said about the return of the Jews to Palestine? What about the rapture and the millenium, and other typical features of books about the end of the world and the second coming of Jesus?

It's time I did some explaining. I am not going to be dragged into long arguments about detailed points of biblical interpretation – there is room for more than one view. But one of the saddest features of many books about the Christian hope is their failure to show how the hope of Christ's return is meant to affect our lives *now*. The books of Daniel and Revelation, which were originally written to comfort God's people in the face of vicious persecution, have become a happy hunting ground for religious extremists. Instead of being sources of hope and encouragement, they have become objects of idle speculation.

So before passing on to discuss how Christian hope can transform our lives, I must briefly give some reasons for taking a different line from many recent writers. Let's look at three well-known areas of speculation – though some readers may prefer to move straight on to chapter eight.

The return of Israel

Many readers will wonder why the return of Jews to Palestine and recent events in Israel received no mention in the chapter on 'Signs of the Times'. Surely this is a most convincing sign – one over which we have every reason to get excited? Hal Lindsey, for example, makes a lot of it in *The Late Great Planet Earth*, which since publication in 1970 has sold over eight million copies. I beg to differ, for several reasons.

To begin with, there is not a whisper about this event in the New Testament. Chapters 9–11 of Paul's Letter to the Romans speaks at length about the destiny of Israel, but Paul's great hope there is for a *spiritual* return of the Jewish people to Christ. Paul says nothing about Jews returning from all over the world to the land of Palestine. In line with Paul, I believe that before the End there will be a substantial turning of Jews to Jesus the Messiah, but there are few signs of that yet.

Of course, there are the Old Testament promises of a return of scattered Jews to the Promised Land. Aren't they good enough, even if the New Testament is silent on the subject? No. Most of them were addressed to Jewish exiles in Babylonia, herded away from Palestine by Nebuchadnezzar after the fall of Jerusalem in 587 B.C. For example, the famous passage about the revival of dry bones in Ezekiel 37 promised to these exiles that God would restore them to Palestine and renew their spiritual and political life. What use would it have been to these depressed exiles in Babylon if Ezekiel had spoken to them of some remote future event which had no relevance to their situation? If Ezekiel was to speak to their need – and all prophets are concerned to do that – he must surely offer some word of comfort, some assurance that God had not forgotten them. That's what he did. His prophecy of a return to Palestine began to be fulfilled in 539 B.C. when the Persian king Cyrus conquered Babylon and ordered the return of all exiles to their homeland.

But that is not to say that Ezekiel's prophecy was *completely* fulfilled in 539 B.C. Ezekiel's hope was for something rather grander than the trickle of returning Jews in the years that followed 539. But the New Testament regularly sees such prophecies come to their fulfilment not in some future restoration of Jews to Palestine, but in the Christian Church. The New Testament often stresses that the Church is now 'the Israel of God' (Galatians 6: 16, NEB). 'If you belong to Christ', it says, 'then you are the descendants of Abraham, and will receive what God has promised' (Galatians 3: 29). What appeared to be a *literal* prophecy in the Old Testament is fulfilled *spiritually* in the New, and what referred to *Jews* in the Old Testament is applied to the *Christian Church* in the New.

In Acts 15 is a record of the Council of Jerusalem (*c.* A.D. 49), where Paul was attacked by some Jewish Christians for welcoming Gentiles into the Church. James, leader of the Jerusalem church, approved of Paul's attitude, and appealed to the prophecy of Amos to support it:

> 'After this I will return, says the Lord,
> And I will raise David's fallen house;
> I will restore its ruins
> And build it up again.
> And so all other people will seek the Lord,
> All the nations whom I have called to be my own.
> So says the Lord, who made this known long ago'
> (Acts 15: 16–18).

Amos was referring to the rebuilding of the Jewish state and the welcome of Gentiles into it. James said this prophecy was being fulfilled as Gentiles entered the Christian Church! And the other apostles present evidently agreed. They weren't always 'literalists', and neither should we be. Now that distinctions between Jew and Gentile are irrelevant, the special significance of Israel's land is irrelevant, even though it seemed crucially important to the Old Testament prophets.

This need not surprise or disturb us. It is a regular feature of Old Testament prophecy, wrote Albertus Pieters, that 'the promises of God to his people are always given in terms of their situation when spoken; but are fulfilled in terms of their situation and needs when the time of fulfilment arrives.' He illustrates it like this. It's as if a wealthy parent, in the 'horse and buggy' days, promised his young son that he should have a horse and buggy on his twenty-first birthday. In the meantime the motor car was invented, so on his twenty-first birthday the son received not a horse and buggy but a car. Now, was the father faithful to his promise? Certainly – wouldn't his son be more delighted than if the promise had been literally fulfilled? [*The Seed of Abraham*, 1950, pp. 127f].

Hal Lindsey stresses the need for a literalistic understanding of prophecy, and describes those who interpret prophecy more figuratively as 'men who cannot believe what is clearly predicted' [*The Late Great Planet Earth*, p .176]. But that is being less than honest. Lindsey himself understands prophecy figuratively when it suits him.

Take, for example, Micah 5:2 which prophesies a coming king who will be born at Bethlehem and will rule over the Jews. Matthew 2:6 sees this fulfilled in the birth of Jesus. But was it *literally* fulfilled? Did Jesus literally become an earthly ruler over the Jewish state, as Micah envisaged? Not at all. He was, and is, a *spiritual* king. Indeed, it was the excessive literalism of Jesus' contemporaries which blinded them to the fact that their true, spiritual ruler and deliverer was in their midst!

And here are two more examples. Lindsey (p. 154) finds in Daniel and Ezekiel prophecies of a war in the Middle East involving Russia. When he finds chariots mentioned as part of the armaments in this war (Daniel 11:40), he refers to them as 'mechanized army'. Why not chariots? Wouldn't 'chariots' mean 'chariots' to the first readers of Daniel? Later (pp. 160f), when he finds Ezekiel describing torrents of fire and brimstone (Ezekiel 38:22), he regards this an an allusion to nuclear weapons (do they contain brimstone?). And he quotes without comment Ezekiel's reference (Ezekiel 39:3) to the bows and arrows of Israel's enemies. Will that be literally fulfilled?

No. The point is that an Old Testament prophet *must* speak in terms which his hearers can understand. But when God later brings the prophecy to fulfilment, it may be on a far grander and more spiritual level than the prophet himself envisaged. So we must always look at Old Testament prophecy *through* the New Testament. And therefore we should conclude that the physical return of Jews to Palestine has no *special* significance in God's purposes. The New Testament encourages us to believe that God's promises to Israel are fulfilled partly in the Christian Church and partly in a *spiritual* turning of Jews to Christ. And that still lies in the future.

There is another serious objection to Hal Lindsey's literalistic view of Old Testament prophecy. Ezekiel 37 promises a return to Palestine not only of Jews from the Southern Kingdom, Judah, who had been removed into exile in Babylonia in 587 B.C. It speaks also of the Northern Kingdom, known as Israel, whose inhabitants had been exiled to the remote provinces of the Assyrian Empire long before in 721 B.C. Ezekiel 37 promises that the scattered people of both the Northern Kingdom – Israel – and the Southern Kingdom – Judah – will return to Palestine where they will be reunited as one nation under one king. This will be clear to anyone who reads Ezekiel 37: 15–28.

So where are these people of the Northern Kingdom now? No one knows. They are the so-called 'Ten Lost Tribes'. When exiled by the Assyrians, they lost their identity as a nation. And we have no means of knowing who their descendants are today – unless you believe, with the British Israelites, that they came to Britain, or with the Mormons that they travelled to America! There is certainly no evidence that descendants of those Israelites exiled to Assyria are among Jews returning to Palestine in the twentieth century. Jews who have settled in Palestine this century are all descendants of the Southern Kingdom, Judah.

That is the trouble with interpreting so many of these prophecies literally – it simply doesn't work. Lindsey has much to say about Ezekiel 37 and the succeeding chapters, but is silent about the problems I have raised. A literal fulfilment of Ezekiel 37 has not happened and is not happening. And if it were to happen we could not tell if it were happening because we have no means of identifying the descendants of the Northern Kingdom. Surely it is preferable to see the prophecy as spiritually fulfilled in the uniting of people of all nations under one king, Jesus.

We may now note briefly other reasons for playing down the significance of current events in Israel. First, the literalism which hopes for the restoration of the Jerusalem temple, with all nations coming to share in its worship and sacrifices (Lindsey, p. 56), is a step backwards, not forwards. The New Testament asserts triumphantly that all such worship and sacrifice has been done away with. It is meaningless. Since Christ died to take away our sins, 'an offering to take away sins is no longer needed' (Hebrews 10: 18).

Secondly, there are more Jews in New York and Moscow than there are in Israel today. Are they all going to return? And thirdly, if we regard Israel's victories in the Palestinian wars since 1948 as the fulfilment of prophecy, we are really giving the Israelis a moral 'blank cheque'. We encourage them to do what they like, however unjust or unreasonable, to Palestinian Arab refugees, Jordanian farmers or Lebanese villagers – all in the name of 'fulfilment of prophecy'. But biblical prophecy is always morally and spiritually conditioned. If a nation 'fulfils prophecy', but does so without regard for the needs and rights of its neighbours, it must answer to the God who hears the cry of the orphan, the widow – and the Arab refugee. Judas fulfilled prophecy, but went to perdition doing so.

Date-fixing by numbers

The desire to fix the time of Christ's return by 'biblical mathematics' has persisted for over a thousand years. There was vast apprehension as the year 1000 approached. Surely the world would end then? But it did not. In the twelfth century an apocalyptic monk named Joachim of Fiore calculated that the present age would end between 1200 and 1260. When Frederick I perished in the Third Crusade in 1190, there began to appear in Germany prophecies of a future Frederick who would liberate Jerusalem from the Moslems and prepare the way for Christ's second coming and the millennium. When Frederick II became emperor and recaptured Jerusalem, the excitement really began. The scene was set for the apocalyptic climax, predicted for 1260. Unfortunately for the theory, in 1250 Frederick suddenly died.

Christopher Columbus, I am told, felt himself commissioned to free Jerusalem from the Moslems and to take the gospel throughout the world in order to pave the way for the millennium. So, in a ship emblazoned with crosses on the sails and 'in the name of Jesus', he set sail – invoking Joachim of Fiore as his patron in the expected evangelization of the world and, inadvertently, in the discovery of the Americas.

John Napier, the inventor of logarithms, used his new-found mathematical techniques to compute the date of Christ's return – between 1688 and 1700. His commentary on the book of Revelation went through twenty-three editions and several translations before 1700. After that, of course, it wasn't quite so convincing. . . .

More recently, Bible students have used various multiples of the number seven, referred to in Daniel and Revelation, to predict the End in 1914 – or various other years of the twentieth century.

The best-known recent estimate was the Jehovah's Witnesses' expectation that the present world system would end in 1975. They had previously announced it for 1874, 1914, 1915 and 1976, but they managed to fiddle the books and keep their movement going. And again in 1975, the world's failure to come to an end led to a quick revision of the calculations.

Now doesn't the divergence of the results produced by all these people, and the fact that so far they've all been wrong, suggest that there's something wrong with the *method*? Does God really intend us to pore over our Bibles with slide-rules and log-tables, and speculate about the date of Christ's return? That wasn't the message that got through to the suffering saints who first read Daniel and Revelation. To them these books were marvellous promises that, despite appearances, God was in control and would bring his plans to completion.

Surely it is only excessive literalism which argues, 'Jesus didn't know the day or the hour of his return, but that doesn't stop us calculating the year and the month'? Jesus' confession of ignorance was genuine. He didn't know when the End would be and rejected the idea that it could be calculated. 'You must be always ready', he said, 'because the Son of Man will come at an hour when you are not expecting him' (Matthew 24: 44).

The numbers in Daniel and Revelation, then, must be understood not literally but symbolically. Often in the Bible the number seven indicates completeness, fulfilment, perfection. So when it is used in these books its purpose is to stress that God *is* in control and he will complete his plans. In *his* good time the kingdom will come to its perfection.

This false hope of calculating the date of the End is not only a theological problem, it is a pastoral problem. Take, for example, those millions of people who have been influenced by Hal Lindsey and similar writers. Many of them are convinced that the present generation is the last generation before the End. In a sense, of course, it is right for every generation to live as though it were the last.

But what if they are wrong to believe that biblical prophecy points to Christ's return within a few years? What if their imagined oasis turns out to be a mirage? Will they still trust the Bible with the same tenacity as they do today, or will 'unfulfilled prophecy' make them disillusioned with it? Some of the first Christians expected an imminent return of Christ. When it didn't happen they were able to cope because they discovered that their Lord

himself was more important than the date of his return.
They learnt to live in hope of his return, and *at the same
time* so to live on the resources of his Holy Spirit that their
faith remained firm even though his return was indefinitely delayed. Can the 'Jesus people' do the same?

St Augustine summed it up like this: 'He who loves the
coming of the Lord is not he who affirms it is far off, nor
is it he who says it is near. It is he who, whether it be far
or near, awaits it with sincere faith, steadfast hope, and
fervent love '

The rapture and the millennium

A view known as 'Dispensational Pre-Millennialism'
commonly adopts the following time-table for the
Final Events:

1. A period of apostasy before Jesus comes.

2. Jesus will come in secret, and will take both dead
and living Christians to be with himself – 'the secret
rapture'.

3. A seven-year period of great tribulation, in which
Antichrist will rule the earth.

4. Then Christ will appear from heaven openly, and
will overthrow Antichrist at Armageddon. This will usher
in Christ's thousand-year reign at Jerusalem, and the
temple and sacrificial worship will be restored.

5. After the thousand years (the 'millennium') Satan
will be loosed again and will stir up rebellion against God.
His crushing defeat will be followed by the resurrection
and judgment of the wicked. Then will follow the final,
eternal state.

A detailed discussion of the drawbacks of this scheme
is given in W. J. Grier's book, *The Momentous Event.*
Here we can only mention the following points.

First, this scheme involves not one future coming of
Christ, but two – surely a deviation from New Testament
teaching. Christ, it argues, will come once for the secret

rapture of the saints, and later to introduce his thousand-year reign. The Scofield Reference Bible tries to defend this view by drawing a completely untenable distinction between 'the day of Christ' and 'the day of the Lord'. In Scripture these clearly refer to the same day.

Second, there is the idea of the secret rapture. It is based mainly on Jesus' words, 'One will be taken away, the other will be left behind' (Matthew 24: 40), coupled with Paul's statement that when Jesus comes believers will rise 'to meet the Lord in the air' (1 Thessalonians 4: 17). This is supposed to mean that Jesus will spirit away those who believe in him, much to the surprise of the unbelievers left behind. Some who accept this theory announce it on car bumper stickers: 'If Jesus returns today, somebody grab my steering wheel'. And there was the American motorist who bought a soft-top car so as not to be hurt on his way up to meet Christ in the air!

But in Matthew 24 there *is* no 'secret rapture'. Jesus' coming will be 'like lightning', 'with power and great glory', and 'the great trumpet will sound' (Matthew 24: 37, 30f). And it is clear in verses 36–44 that judgment will take place *at the same time* as salvation. The theory of two comings of Christ – one in secret and one in public – is a myth.

What's more, it is a myth invented by J. N. Darby, who founded the Exclusive Brethren towards the middle of the nineteenth century. Its pedigree is no older than that, despite its popularity today.

Thirdly, the idea that Christian believers will escape the 'Great Tribulation' contradicts the New Testament's insistence that Jesus' followers are preserved not from suffering but *through* suffering. 'We must pass through many troubles to enter the kingdom of God' (Acts 14: 22).

Fourthly, the idea of a thousand-year reign appears in the Bible only in Revelation 20. That is no reason for dismissing it, but it is a hint that the millennium is not to be regarded as a literal thousand-year reign on earth. Jesus, Paul and the other New Testament writers sometimes divide the whole of time into two ages – the present age and the age to come (e.g., Mark 10: 30; Ephesians 1: 21). This leaves no room for a millennial age in between. There are two ages, divided by the single event of Christ's coming, the resurrection and the judgment.

So how should we understand the passage about the millennium in Revelation 20: 1–6? Certainly we should note that there is no mention of a reign *on earth*. If the 'thrones' (verse 4) are anywhere, they are in heaven, like all the other thrones mentioned in Revelation (except for the thrones of Satan and of 'the beast'). It is better to understand this thousand-year reign not as some future literal, earthly reign, but as a symbol of the period between Christ's resurrection and final coming. John is giving us a peep behind the scenes, to show us that despite the persecution of God's people, Christ is not defeated, nor are those who have been martyred for his sake.

'The Lord, our Almighty God, is King!'

Revelation is a book of confusing symbols and complicated patterns. Yet its basic message is the message of God's triumph, and we neglect that to our loss. It was written at the end of the first century, in the time of the Roman Emperor Domitian. Claiming to be God, he exercised a cruel tyranny over his people. And Christians were suffering persecution. The book was written for them, as a glimpse into the way God is working. People were asking, 'Where is God in all this? Who is in control? Does power lie in the hands of God, or of Domitian?' And today the same question is asked – 'Where does power lie? Is it in Moscow, or Peking, or somewhere else?'

Back comes the triumphant reply: 'The Lord, our Almighty God, is King.' (Revelation 19: 6). That's where the power lies, despite all appearances to the contrary. That's where you can find your security, even when you hear the boots of the guards coming to take you from your cell to the firing-squad.

This is no armchair theologian's glib answer to the problem. It is the answer which God revealed to a man who was himself suffering exile like the exile of Siberia, because of his faith in Christ (Revelation 1: 9). He knows that God has not abandoned his people in their torment. He has not abandoned history to the powers of evil. How does he know? Because God has acted in history! At the centre of history stands the cross of the slaughtered Lamb, the Lamb who has conquered by his love. He says, 'I am the first and the last. I am the living one! I was dead, but look, I am alive for ever and ever. I have authority over death and the world of the dead' (Revelation 1: 17f).

Whatever the power of evil may do to the followers of the Lamb, it cannot snatch them from their reigning Lord, who promises them a share in his 'new heaven and new earth'. His reign will not always remain hidden, for he promises, 'I am coming soon! ' – to make his reign complete among men. And the only fitting response is 'So be it. Come, Lord Jesus! ' (Revelation 22: 20).

For further reading

W. J. Grier, *The Momentous Event* (Banner of Truth, 1970)

H. Lindsey, *The Late Great Planet Earth* (Lakeland, 1971)

8

LIVING BETWEEN THE TIMES

Nowhere in the Bible is there an organized, straight-forward account of the doctrine of the return of Christ. If there were, this book would have been easier to write – or unnecessary! And there wouldn't be so many disagreements among Bible students over the details of the doctrine. But why is there no such detailed account? Because the hope of Christ's return is not a dogma to tickle our brains, but a fact to change our lives. Whenever the Bible speaks about Christ's second coming its purpose is always to challenge us to action. So when the biblical writers refer to it, their purpose is not to give a detailed explanation of the doctrine, but to relate it to practical needs. When we really see how this hope is meant to affect our lives, we can never be the same again.

We are living 'between the times' – between the time when Jesus introduced God's new era and the time when he will return to establish God's kingdom in its final form. Waiting for that momentous event is not a matter of sitting in our back gardens with our telescopes scanning the horizon. It is not a matter of killing time like waiting for a late train. It is a time for action, a time for distinctive Christian living. Let's look at some of the ways in which our hope should affect our lives.

The forward look

The first thing the Christian hope does is to smite firmly on the head the idea that Christian piety consists in longing for a repeat performance of some past Golden Age.

That's just a form of sanctified escapism. While our next-door neighbour queues up for his tickets for *The Good Old Days*, we take a journey down Memory Lane to 'the night when I was converted' or 'the days when we had five hundred in the Sunday School'. Or further back still to the Evangelical Revival or the golden age of the Puritans.

Of course, a study of church history could do us all good, and it can be valuable to look to the past in order to take stock of the present situation. But, as Colin Morris insists in *The Hammer of the Lord*, you can't go *back* to God. God is always up front, calling us forward, not back to the good old days. And God is not so uncreative as to offer us simply repeat performances of past wonders. He is always doing some new wonder, leading his people forward into some new Promised Land, some new activity of his incredible grace. He thrust Abraham out from the security of Mesopotamia on a journey to an unknown destination, with just a few relatives, a few sheep and the odd camel – and a promise: 'I will make you into a great nation, I will bless you and make your name great, so that you will be a blessing' (Genesis 12: 2). He pushed the Israelites out of Egypt into a strange and unpromising desert – and when things got tough some of them longed to be back in the security of Egyptian slavery rather than go forward on God's adventure into the future. God brought Jesus through the dead end of the cross to the new beginning of the empty tomb. He allowed the early Jerusalem church to suffer persecution so that they would flee from the city and begin the worldwide proclamation of the gospel (Acts 8: 1–4).

God leads us forward, not back. The Christian life means looking forward to the coming of Christ, like runners straining for the finishing tape.

Pilgrim's progress

Another thing the Bible says about Abraham and all true men of faith is that they are pilgrims – people who are just passing travellers, because they have no permanent home on earth. These men 'admitted openly that they were foreigners and refugees (or "pilgrims") on earth. . . . Their thought did not go back to the country they had left; in that case they would have had the chance to return. Instead, it was a better country they longed for, the heavenly country. And so God is not ashamed to have them call him their God, for he has prepared a city for them' (Hebrews 11: 13–16). The real reason for the forward look we have just mentioned is that ultimately we don't *belong* on the earth as it is. We are 'citizens of *heaven*' (Philippians 3: 20). Heaven is our goal, and that affects all our values.

Someone has said that the twentieth century Church is 'the best-disguised set of pilgrims the world has ever seen'. What signs do we give that we don't ultimately belong here but are just 'passing through', when for many of us the only mark of real sacrifice is that we don't get our colour television until a year or two after our next-door neighbour got his? There is, of course, a certain security to be found in going through life, like a snail or a tortoise, with all the necessities of life attached firmly to us. But neither snails nor tortoises are famous for their speed or manoeuvrability.

Now I am not saying that the only way to be a decent Christian is to become a hermit. Jesus himself had a most vivid sense that the End might break in at any moment: yet he spent enough time enjoying his food and drink to acquire the reputation of being 'a glutton and a wine-drinker' (Matthew 11: 19). His parables show keen perception and sensitivity towards the world of nature – because he knew that even though our goal is beyond this world, *this world is still God's world*. All this is quite different from the world-denying apocalyptic of sects like the Jehovah's Witnesses.

There is, then, a proper tension in the Christian life. We are in the world but not of it. We enjoy this world as God's gift, but we don't ultimately belong here, and God may bring human history to an end at any moment. Paul expressed this tension in his correspondence with his friend Timothy. In his first letter he wrote, 'Everything that God has created is good; nothing is to be rejected, but all is to be received with a prayer of thanks' (1 Timothy 4: 4). But later he made it clear that followers of Jesus should not cling to the good things of earthly life: 'Take your part in suffering, as a loyal soldier of Jesus Christ. A soldier in active service does not get mixed up in the affairs of civilian life, because he wants to please his commanding officer' (2 Timothy 2: 3f).

So the hope that Jesus is coming soon does *not* mean that we give up our normal pattern of life. Paul did not mince words with people who gave up their jobs because they thought Christ's return was just round the corner: 'The man who will not work shall not eat' (2 Thessalonians 3: 10, NEB). And Luther said that if he knew the world would end tomorrow, his duty today would still require him to plant his garden – and to collect the rent! There is nothing wrong with planning for the future.

And yet we must never plan as though our future on earth were the only future there is. And that's where we often go wrong. Take the question of money, for example. Our society is riddled with materialistic values – witness the alluring adverts that confront you on page after page of weekend colour supplements and women's magazines. To my mind the long-term effects of these encouragements to covetousness are far more damaging than any X-film. Yet how many Christians show by their lives their belief that 'a man's true life is not made up of the things he owns' (Luke 12: 15)?

Christianity Today for 11th May 1973 reported that a men's dormitory for an Indian theological college, half-finished in 1956, had not been completed till 1971 because of lack of funds. The amount in question was less than 10,000 dollars. 'That is, we have heard, the amount of the purse paid to a Christian celebrity to accompany over three hundred tourists on a jumbo jet to Israel: "the largest airborne pilgrimage in history".'

C. S. Lewis said that the doctrine that Christ is coming is unpopular because it cuts across the plans and dreams of millions of people. They want to make their plans for a comfortable future, they want to amass their fortunes. And Jesus called them fools. For, he said, when the End comes, 'who will get all these things you have kept for yourself?' (Luke 12: 20).

And what about the institutional life of the Church? In the Middle Ages the Church's very success caused it to imagine that it was building the City of God on earth, and it took to itself the authority of that City. But if we are pilgrims, if our destiny is beyond this present age, if God is always calling us forward, we *dare* not allow the Church to be an unchanging institution with vested interests and fossilized structures. Consider this story about Ignatius of Loyola. When a friend asked him how he would feel if the pope dissolved the Society of Jesus – the religious order which Ignatius had spent so much time and energy to establish – he replied, 'A quarter of an hour's prayer, and I should think no more about it'.

When Jesus comes all our human institutions, including Christian ones, will come to an end. We would do well to take that into account. A truly biblical church will build for future generations, but it will never build as though the future belonged to it by right. And it will fervently pray for the day when the Church itself will become the transformed community of heaven.

Life in the Spirit

Living 'between the times' isn't only a matter of knowing that one day the End will come. There are some things we don't have to wait for. The Holy Spirit is God's gift to his people *now*. To understand the significance of this we must see how the New Testament describes the Holy Spirit.

'The Spirit', Paul wrote, 'is the *guarantee* that we shall receive what God has promised his people' (Ephesians

1: 14). In Greek this word 'guarantee' means an advance payment or a first instalment – a part-payment which is a pledge that in due course the full payment will be made. Some interesting examples of the use of this word have survived on some ancient Greek business contracts written on papyrus. According to one of these contracts, a woman sold a cow and received a thousand *drachmas* as a down-payment or 'guarantee' that in due time the rest of the purchase price would be paid. Another contract concerns a troop of castanet-playing dancing girls who were engaged for a village fête. They were paid so many *drachmas* in advance as a down-payment or 'guarantee', on the understanding that an additional payment would be made after the performance.

In a similar way, says Paul, the Holy Spirit is your down-payment or first instalment of the life of heaven – the guarantee that the full experience of heaven will follow at some future time. The Holy Spirit gives a foretaste of heaven – only a foretaste, but a real taste nonetheless. The Spirit is God's power in the Church, enabling us to *demonstrate the life of heaven on earth.* In chapter two we saw how Jesus demonstrated that the reign of God had begun in his ministry. How did he do it? By the power of the Spirit at work in him! His sermon at Nazareth began with these words from Isaiah:

'*The Spirit of the Lord is upon me.*
He has anointed me to preach the good news to the poor,
He has sent me to proclaim liberty to the captives,
And recovery of sight to the blind,
To set free the oppressed,
To announce the year when the Lord will save his people!' (Luke 4: 18f).

And when challenged by the Pharisees about his exorcisms he replied, 'It is *God's Spirit* who gives me the power to drive out demons, which proves that the kingdom of God has already come upon you' (Matthew 12: 28).

By the Holy Spirit's power Jesus showed what God's kingdom is like – evil forces are defeated, disease and death are overcome, the poor and the outcast are precious to God. And at Pentecost the power of this same Spirit was unleashed in the Church. And ever since, he has been driving out demons, healing sick bodies, liberating men from evil habits, moral defeat and the power of guilt. He has been giving foretastes of heaven.

If, then, we are to live as 'citizens of heaven', we must give scope to the Spirit and his gifts. But there are other ways, too, in which God's Spirit enables us to demonstrate the life of heaven.

First, he is *the creator of community*. In heaven God's people will live in a harmonious community – with God himself at the centre – and the Holy Spirit can begin to make that a reality *now*. One of the marvellous things about Pentecost was the way in which people from different nations were drawn together. Age-old barriers between Jew and Gentile were shattered as the Spirit of love laid hold of men's lives. A new quality of community was born. 'All of us, Jews and Gentiles, slaves and free men, have been baptized into the one body by the same Spirit, and we have all been given the same Spirit to drink' (1 Corinthians 12: 13). Sadly, this community is still fragile and imperfect. But to think of it as the foretaste of the heavenly community should help us to get things into perspective. For example, there are some churches and denominations which deny the validity of other churches' communion services, or refuse to welcome other Christians to their own communion services. Might they not look rather silly when all God's people share together in the 'wedding feast' of Christ – that feast of which the communion service is meant to be a foretaste?

At any rate, our witness to the reality of heaven will not be taken seriously in the world unless we show some signs of belonging to a community which transcends the barriers of race and class – a community committed to costly caring for each other. When the Church strives after that ideal, it is a symbol of hope.

A second way in which the Holy Spirit enables us to demonstrate the life of heaven is by *making us more like Christ*. The traditional word for this is 'holiness', but what is holiness if is isn't Christ-likeness? Let's look again at a passage we have already noted: 'My dear friends, we are now God's children, but it is not yet clear what we shall become. But this we know: when Christ appears, we shall become like him, because we shall see him as he really is.' But the writer goes on: 'Everyone who has this hope in Christ keeps himself pure, just as Christ is pure' (1 John 3: 2f). Because we are *already* citizens of heaven and *already* children of God, we should increasingly be revealing the 'family likeness' and showing signs of the purity which we shall share with Christ in heaven.

This increasing Christ-likeness becomes possible as we lay ourselves open to the influence of the Spirit: 'We all reflect as in a mirror the splendour of the Lord; thus we are transfigured into his likeness, from splendour to splendour; such is the influence of the Lord who is the Spirit' (2 Corinthians 3: 18).

What does it mean in practice to be like Christ? Turn up almost any page of the New Testament and you have food enough for thought – and action. Jesus stands out as one who came to serve rather than to be served, to do his Father's will rather than his own, to give up his life for others rather than to save his own skin. His way of life was so different from popular twentieth century attitudes that we can't fail to be noticed if we seriously try to follow his pattern. We may be sneered at as well as noticed, but who in his right mind would deny that the way of Christ is infinitely better and truer than simply looking after number one? Think over, for example, the following pasages:

'If anyone wants to come with me, he must forget himself, carry his cross, and follow me. For the man who wants to save his own life will lose it; but the man who loses his life for me and for the gospel will save it. Does a man gain anything if he wins the whole world but loses his life? Of course not! There is nothing a man can give to regain his life' (Mark 8: 34–37).

'Happy are those who know they are spiritually poor:
    the kingdom of heaven belongs to them!
Happy are those who mourn:
    God will comfort them!
Happy are the meek:
    they will receive what God has promised!
Happy are those whose greatest desire is to do what God
    requires:
    God will satisfy them fully!
Happy are those who show mercy to others:
    God will show mercy to them!
Happy are the pure in heart:
    they will see God!
Happy are those who work for peace among men:
    God will call them his sons!
Happy are those who suffer persecution because they do
    what God requires:
    the kingdom of heaven belongs to them!
Happy are you when men insult you and mistreat you and tell all kinds of evil lies against you because you are my followers. Rejoice and be glad, because a great reward is kept for you in heaven. This is how men mistreated the prophets who lived before you' (Matthew 5: 3–12).

'You have heard that it was said, "Love your friends, hate your enemies". But now I tell you: love your enemies, and pray for those who mistreat you, so that you will become the sons of your Father in heaven. For he makes his sun to shine on bad and good people alike, and gives rain to those who do right and those who do wrong. Why should you expect God to reward you, if you love only the people who love you? Even the tax collectors do that! And if you speak only to your friends, have you done anything out of the ordinary? Even the pagans do that! You must be perfect – just as your Father in heaven is perfect' (Matthew 5: 43–48).

To live by those principles is to demonstrate that there's more to man's life than his seventy years and his bank balance. It is to bear witness to the life of heaven.

The third way in which the Spirit enables us to bear this witness is in *worship*. Heaven will resound with the worship of God's people, but the Church on earth can anticipate that worship now. 'It is through Christ that all of us, Jews and Gentiles, are able to come *in the one Spirit* into the presence of the Father' (Ephesians 2: 18). In worship we look forward to the coming of God's kingdom, and we get beyond the restrictions of time to join our worship with the worship of the saints in heaven. This is what the writer to the Hebrews meant when he wrote: '*You have come* to Mount Zion and to the city of the living God, the heavenly Jerusalem, with its thousands of angels. *You have come* to the joyful gathering of God's oldest sons, whose names are written in heaven. *You have come* to God, who is the Judge of all men, and to the spirits of righteous men made perfect. *You have come* to Jesus . . .' (Hebrews 12: 22–24).

If this is true of all Christian worship it is true especially of the Lord's Supper, in which we 'proclaim the Lord's death *until he comes*' (1 Corinthians 11: 26). As we meet with Jesus at the communion table, we experience a fore-taste of the richer fellowship of his final kingdom.

'Living between the times', then, means looking forward to God's future, like runners straining for the finishing tape. It means living as pilgrims on the earth. It means living in the power of the Holy Spirit – being 'citizens of heaven' who show where we really belong. But it is not only in these ways that the hope of Christ's return can affect our lives. We shall see more in the next chapter.

For further reading

E. M. B. Green, *New Life, New Lifestyle* (Hodder, 1973)

M. C. Griffiths, *Take my Life* (IVP, 1967)

B. Milne, *We Belong Together* (IVP, 1978)

*J. V. Taylor, *The Go-Between God: the Holy Spirit and the Christian Mission* (SCM, 1972)

Questions for Discussion

1. Does your church and its individual members give the impression of being 'pilgrims'? What practical changes might you make in order to live more like 'pilgrims'?

2. How can we become more open to the Holy Spirit's work in the Church's worship and community life?

3. How can your church or group 'bear witness to the life of heaven' in such a way that other people can *see* your witness?

4. Study Matthew 5: 3–12. What qualities does Jesus expect in his followers? Think of some examples of how these qualities should be expressed in practice. Where appropriate, contrast them with popular modern attitudes. What promises does Jesus give to those who show these qualities?

9

THE END IS NOT YET

The Holy Spirit, then, enables us to demonstrate the life of heaven. We can bear witness to the fact that we are citizens of heaven, but the fact remains that the heavenly city still lies in the future. Pilgrim is still progressing. This fact gives us six more hints about the nature of Christian living.

A life of prayer

First, Christian life is a life of prayer. Consider for a moment the first part of the Lord's Prayer:

> 'Our Father in heaven,
> Thy name be hallowed;
> Thy kingdom come,
> Thy will be done,
> On earth as in heaven' (Matthew 6: 9f).

If God's final kingdom is something which he himself will bring, and not something which men can achieve, then the most significant thing we can do to prepare for its coming is to pray. When we pray like this we are saying, in effect: 'Father, we long for you to receive the honour that is your due. We long for the day when your kingdom of righteousness shall be finally established, and men shall love to do your will. This is something only you can bring to reality. But we believe that, as we live in dependence on you, we may experience in part the blessings of your final kingdom.'

So it is that *sometimes* God's name is hallowed, *some-*

times God's will is done. But God will not receive the full honour of which he is worthy, nor will his will be perfectly done, until Jesus comes to establish his final kingdom. And in all our prayers we experience this tension. When, for instance, we pray for peace between nations, we trust God to restrain men's hatred and national aggression. Yet we know that our prayer will be completely answered only when Jesus returns, because wars and unrest are an inevitable part of the world scene until then. There are many prayers for which the only *complete* answer is the return of Christ.

Spiritual warfare

Secondly, to live as a Christian means unceasing involvement in spiritual warfare. We saw in chapter three that although Jesus has triumphed over evil powers, the victory will not be complete until he comes again. When the end comes 'Christ will overcome all spiritual rulers, authorities, and powers, and hand over the kingdom to God the Father. For Christ must rule until God defeats all enemies and puts them under his feet' (1 Corinthians 15: 24f). Not till then shall we be free from temptation and the smell of battle.

Meanwhile there's no time for spiritual picnicking and gospel entertainment. There's a war on. 'We are not fighting against human beings, but against the wicked spiritual forces in the heavenly world, the rulers, authorities, and cosmic powers of this dark age. So take up God's armour now! Then when the evil day comes, you will be able to resist the enemy's attacks, and after fighting to the end, you will still hold your ground' (Ephesians 6: 12f). Unless we have a real sense of battle, we shall have no sense of urgency in the fight – and no sense of victory.

If we know there's a battle on, we shall be able to understand better some of the things we experience in our own lives. Why is it so hard to do God's will even when we know what it is? Why do we so often fail? Is there something wrong with us if we feel the power of temptation coming a us stronger than ever? No, it's perfectly normal. We experience this agonizing tension just because we are 'living between the times'. We belong to God's kingdom, and yet we still live in 'this present evil age' (Galatians 1: 4). And so the battle between God and Satan, good and evil, rages *inside us*. It's like being caught in the cross-fire between two opposing armies. Or it's like the pain we feel when we come from a walk in the frosty air into a warm room. Our ears and hands tingle as cold confronts warmth. The sensation is not pleasant, but we endure it cheerfully because we know it's *better* to be warm than cold.

This conflict that rages inside us is discussed by Paul in Romans 7 and Galatians 5:

'So I find that this law is at work: when I want to do what is good, what is evil is the only choice I have. My inner being delights in the law of God. But I see a different law at work in my body – a law that fights against the law that my mind approves of. It makes me a prisoner to the law of sin which is at work in my body. What an unhappy man I am! Who will rescue me from this body that is taking me to death? Thanks be to God, through our Lord Jesus Christ! This, then, is my condition: by myself I can serve God's law only with my mind, while my human nature serves the law of sin' (Romans 7: 21–25).

So there *is* deliverance from the grip of evil – that is God's promise through Jesus. But there will be no deliverance from *temptation* to evil until the 'body that is taking me to death' is transformed into the resurrection body. How, then, do we cope with the present situation? Let Paul answer for himself:

'Let the Spirit direct your lives, and you will not satisfy the desires of the human nature. For what our human nature wants is opposed to what the Spirit wants, and what the Spirit wants is opposed to what human nature wants: the two are enemies, and this means that you cannot do what you want to do. If the Spirit leads you, then you are not subject to the Law' (Galatians 5:16–18).

If we are engaged in warfare, with no complete and final victory until Christ comes again, we must beware of any brand of Christianity which gives the impression of 'having arrived'. There is no formula for instant success in the battle, *no* level of Christian life which puts you beyond temptation. And any kind of spirituality which makes such claims – whether it calls itself 'charismatic' or 'perfection-ist' or by any other name – is a false hope. The Holy Spirit does grant decisive spiritual victories in the lives of God's people, but there is no final victory, no end to the battle, until the end of this present age.

A life of faith

That brings us to the third point: the Christian life is a life of faith. That may seem obvious, but it needs saying because we all have a natural craving to escape from the uncertainties of faith into the comfortable security of sight. We want to know the date of Christ's return, we want God to give us some infallible sign that his coming is just round the corner, we want God to deal with all our unanswered questions about the future. But Christian life can't be like that. 'Our life is a matter of faith, not of sight' (2 Corinthians 5: 7). 'What we see now is like the dim image in a mirror; then (when Christ returns) we shall see face to face. What I know now is only partial; then it will be complete, as complete as God's knowledge of me' (1 Corinthians 13: 12). That promise is both marvellous and challenging. Because we know that God has prepared for us a 'city' where faith will give way to sight, we can live with all the uncertainties and unanswered questions of our present life. To know the future and to know the answers to all our questions is less vital for us than to be known and loved by God, who holds our future in his hands.

A life of evangelism

The gospel of hope is a message to share, and a man must either give away Christianity or give it up. Evangelism is one of the marks of the whole period between Jesus' resurrection and his return: 'Before the end the gospel must be proclaimed to all nations' (Mark 13: 10, NEB). God's Church in every generation has the job of declaring Christ's Lordship and offering his forgiveness to every nation. Jesus gave no assurance that the gospel would be *believed* by all men, but he did say it would be *proclaimed*.

When the risen Christ spoke with his apostles they asked if the time had come for the final establishing of God's kingdom. Jesus replied: 'The times and occasions are set by my Father's own authority, and it is not for you to know when they will be. But you will be filled with power when the Holy Spirit comes on you, and you will be witnesses for me in Jerusalem, in all of Judea and Samaria, and to the ends of the earth' (Acts 1: 7f). A few days later the Spirit was poured out and the mission began. Notice that Jesus here did not *command* his followers to be his witnesses, he *promised* they would be, as the Holy Spirit drove them forward. And that's what happened.

You will not find many exhortations to evangelism in the New Testament – for the most part the writers simply assume that the gospel is being shared and people are coming to faith. The first century churches had many problems, but stagnation in evangelism was not one of them.

We easily forget that the last hundred years have seen a greater advance of the Church's mission than any previous century. In tropical Africa the Church is growing at the rate of six per cent a year. In South America and Indonesia it is ten per cent a year. At a church synod in Indonesia it was seriously suggested that baptisms should cease for a year or two to give the church time to catch up with what God is doing!

If heaven is open to men 'from every tribe, and language, and people, and nation', then God's mission is worldwide.

And if the Church is interested in heaven, it must be interested in worldwide mission. There was a time when the Holy Spirit told the worshipping church in Antioch to send two of its leading members, Paul and Barnabas, on a mission tour of Cyprus and Turkey. What if the church there had protested: 'But, Lord, these are gifted men and we need them for all the work there is to do here'? The mission would not have advanced, and the church would have been resisting the Holy Spirit. A church which closes its heart to the call of the Spirit will make no impact on its own neighbourhood or further afield. A church that is dedicated to mission and willing to share its manpower is open to the powerful blessing of the Spirit.

Is this one reason why many of our churches are so weak in their witness – resistance to the Holy Spirit? Everyone talks these days about the problems of communication, and I certainly do my fair share of that. But this kind of talk *can* become an excuse for refusing to face three basic reasons for our frequent failure to communicate.

First, we are uncertain about *what* we have to communicate. A few years ago there was a newspaper cartoon showing the runner from Marathon, as the ancient Greek story presents him. He arrives gasping and falls prostrate before the king. A blank look comes over his face and he mumbles, 'I've forgotten the message'. A church which is uncertain or which compromises the Christian message – as it is outlined, for example, in chapter two above – will not only be ineffective. It will be resisting the Spirit of truth.

Secondly, we are uncertain about *who* is meant to do the communicating. We assume it's the minister's job – that's what we pay him for! That isn't how it was in the early church. When persecution arose in Jerusalem the believers scattered all over Palestine – *'except the apostles'* (Acts 8: 1). And wherever they went the message went with them and churches were born.

Of course, not all of us have the gift of being evangelists, but all of us are witnesses. And witnessing involves living a life that commends Christ and saying what Christ means to us when opportunities arise. Kenneth Strachan, pioneer of the 'Evangelism in Depth' method, said: 'The growth of any movement is in direct proportion to the success of that movement in mobilizing its total membership for the propagation of its beliefs.' Yet how many churches do you know which function on that basis? How many churches do you know where systematic training for mission is given? If we fail in this, are we not resisting the Spirit who creates the body of Christ and distributes his gifts to his people?

Thirdly, we fail because we are unwilling for the cost of love. When all's said and done, what really communicates is not clever methods but *people*. What really 'comes over' is the kind of person you are – your sincerity, your integrity, your love, your dedication to the Christ you believe in. How has God communicated to us? Not just by talking to us, but by living a real life amongst us in the person of Jesus. That is our model: 'As the Father sent me', said Jesus, 'so I send you' (John 20: 21). To take that seriously means spending ourselves in loving and caring about people, and that's costly. Sharing people's interests, their joys, their problems, their sufferings – that's costly. But that's love. Normal evangelism arises naturally from living in relationship with people.

Scores of methods of evangelism may be useful *alongside* this living in relationship. But if we use methods of evangelism *without* being willing to live in relationship to people, to win their trust and show them the love of Christ, we shall not be following the Holy Spirit's method. We shall be resisting the Spirit of love. Our mission will be ineffective because we were unwilling for the demands of loving relationships.

The vision of heaven where people of all races and all times will live in relationship with each other, all worshipping the one Christ, is a marvellous encouragement to world evangelism. 'So then, my dear brothers, stand firm and steady. Keep busy always in your work for the Lord, since you know that what you do in the Lord's service is never wasted' (1 Corinthians 15: 58).

A life of service

God's mission doesn't mean only drawing people into his kingdom. It means serving and caring about people of all kinds – just because they are people whom God created and loves. In Matthew's Gospel the last recorded teaching of Jesus' earthly life is a Judgment scene (Matthew 25: 31–46). Jesus the King will divide all the earth's people into two groups. To one group he will say: 'You who are blessed by my Father: come! Come and receive the kingdom which has been prepared for you ever since the creation of the world. I was hungry and you fed me, thirsty and you gave me drink; I was a stranger and you received me in your homes, naked and you clothed me; I was sick and you took care of me, in prison and you visited me. . . .'

Jesus, the suffering Son of Man, identifies with all who suffer and are in need, and says to us: 'You show your attitude to me by the way you react to your fellow-men in their suffering. On that basis you will be judged.' Notice that it is not positive wrongdoing which Jesus condemns, but utter failure to do good. Living as a Christian means not just keeping away from evil influences, but showing the compassion of Christ for all whose needs confront us.

How are we to react to this description of the judgment? Must we not say, 'I haven't been too good at loving people like this. Yet that is how seriously God treats these deeds of love'? At the judgment God will ignore many of the things which men consider great and lasting. The greatest glories of this world will burst like soap bubbles, and the smallest acts of love will be magnified to their true perspective.

No one could put it plainer than John: 'If a man is rich and sees his brother in need, yet closes his heart against his brother, how can he claim that he has love for God in his heart? My children! Our love should not be just words

and talk; it must be true love, which shows itself in action'
(1 John 3: 17f).

'The world will make you suffer'

One final thing about living in the present age: Jesus
promised suffering for his Church. Like Winston Churchill
offering 'blood, toil, tears and sweat', Jesus was utterly
realistic. 'If the world hates you', he said, 'you must remember that it has hated me first. If you belonged to the
world, then the world would love you as its own. But I
chose you from this world, and you do not belong to it;
this is why the world hates you' (John 15: 18f).
   Is this a word to the Church today? In our search for
'success' we have forgotten the call to suffer, and the
promise that true success in Christian work comes only
through suffering. And the kind of success that does come
through suffering tends to be very different from the
shallow success we often seek. The pattern for us is the
same as it was for our Lord: 'A grain of wheat is no more
than a single grain unless it is dropped into the ground
and dies. If it does die, then it produces many grains' (John
12: 24).
   'When Christ calls a man', wrote Bonhoeffer, 'he bids
him come and die'. Becoming a Christian doesn't lead to a
superficial happiness and an instant solution to all problems. It leads to costly obedience and a life which involves
suffering. James and John once asked Jesus if he would
grant them the best seats in heaven. 'You don't know what
you're asking for', replied Jesus. 'Can you drink the cup
that I must drink?' – can you go through the suffering that
I have to go through? (Mark 10: 38). Jesus could promise
suffering, but God alone can decide who sits where in
heaven.
   So suffering is the order of the day. For a Christian in
Russia it meant three years imprisonment. His crime? He
had said grace at a children's party. For converts from
Islam in many countries it means the constant threat of

being poisoned by their Moslem friends. For Martin Luther King it meant hatred from whites and criticism from many blacks as he pursued to the end the cause of non-violent revolution. For us it might mean losing a job because we can't condone shady practices in business. It may mean hostility from our workmates or schoolmates. It may mean the pain of divisions in the family because others don't share our faith. It may mean the heartache of bearing other people's sorrows and problems.

But it will not be wasted. True, 'we must pass through many troubles to enter the kingdom of God' (Acts 14: 22). But we shall get there! And we shall take others along with us. For suffering has creative power. There have been more Christian martyrs in the last hundred years than at any other period of church history – and there has been more church growth too.

Leonard Wilson, who later became Bishop of Birmingham, was tortured by the Japanese during World War II. When the Japanese asked him why, if he believed in God, God did not save him, he answered, 'God doesn't save people from punishment or pain. He saves them by giving them the strength and the spirit to bear it.' Later he went back to baptize one of his torturers – a man who had come to share Bishop Wilson's faith in Christ because of the way Christ had strengthened him through suffering.

'The world will make you suffer', Jesus warned. But what were his next words? 'Take courage! I have defeated the world! ' (John 16: 33). And how did he do that? Not by a show of force or by spiritual entertainment, but by giving himself, in life and death, for the sake of others. And the way of Christ is the way for his followers – through suffering to the glory of his kingdom.

But most of us in Britain don't suffer very much for our faith. What are we to do about that? Certainly the New Testament does not encourage us to go out looking for trouble. On the contrary, it urges us to 'live at peace with all men' and 'obey the state authorities' (Romans 12, 13). We aren't called to go looking for suffering, but we *are* called to be Christ-like. Now why did Jesus suffer? He got into hot water because he challenged injustice, he loved the outcast, he threatened the nation's power structures, he was too uncomfortable to live with, he spoke the truth and it hurt, he took on his shoulders the oppressive weight of evil. That's why he suffered, and that is the pattern for us. If we genuinely aim to become like him we shall inevitably find ourselves getting into hot water as he did. We don't need to go out asking for suffering – we shall find it coming to us if we really seek to follow Jesus in every area of our lives.

'All who want to live a godly life in union with Christ Jesus will be persecuted' (2 Timothy 3: 12). But they *will* be 'in union with Christ Jesus', and that is the deepest consolation.

For further reading

E. M. B. Green, *Evangelism: Now and Then* (IVP, 1979)

G. Appleton, *The Practice of Prayer* (Mowbrays, 1979)

P. Little, *How to Give Away Your Faith* (IVP, 1971)

R. M. Pippert, *Out of the Saltshaker* (IVP, 1980)

D. C. K. Watson, *I Believe in Evangelism* (Hodder, 1976)

Questions for Discussion

1. Do we take seriously enough the idea of the Christian life as spiritual warfare? Can you give examples from personal experience of what this warfare involves?

2. Do you agree with the 'three basic reasons for our failure to communicate' which are suggested in this chapter? What can you do to overcome them?

3. Draw up an outline for a training programme in evangelism and service for your church or group. On what subjects do you need teaching? After some basic training, what practical projects could you undertake?
4. Study 1 Thessalonians 2: 1–20. What can we learn from Paul's example about our attitudes and methods in evangelism and in building up young Christians?

10

THE KINGDOM OF GOD ON EARTH?

Christian hope offers the breathtaking prospect of life in the presence of God after the return of Christ. It provides both guidelines and a dynamic for living the Christian life. But is that all? What about society as a whole? Does Christian hope include the idea of the improvement of human society? And what about all the problems we mentioned in chapter one? When I wrote that, was I doing the old trick of filling people with doom so that they would be receptive to the offer of an escape route? Are we simply to ignore those problems and wait for the day when we shall escape from the tragedies and tensions of life?

It is clear from the Bible that there will be no earthly utopia of the sort sometimes expected by naïve visionaries and misguided Christians. The kingdom of God is not an earthly paradise which the Church can 'spread' like jam or 'set up' like a committee. The kingdom is God's act, and it will not come in its perfection until Jesus returns in glory. But, equally clearly, the Bible gives no warrant for opting out and abandoning the world to destruction, like rats leaving a sinking ship. Some Christians denounce the mounting evils in society in such a way that you suspect that they are secretly gloating over the increase of evil, because they regard it as a sure sign of the Lord's imminent return.

That is not the Christian way. The early Christians knew Jesus might come at any time, yet they did much to break down the barriers between races and between slaves and free men. They met the needs of widows and provided for famine relief. All this they did at a time when they had no political power at all. For us in our own day to opt out of involvement in social change – *when we have some answers* – is worse than the escapism of the bewildered and the helpless to whom we referred in chapter one.

But why should we be involved in social and political action? Is it not enough to proclaim the gospel and to care for those in need? Here are some reasons why we can't opt out.

Motives for social action

In the first place, it is naïve to assume that all you need is new men and you will automatically get a new society. Nowhere in the world has there been such consistent 'gospel-preaching' as in Northern Ireland, South Africa and the southern states of America. But if the preaching has no social content, how will your 'new men' begin to change society's structures in order to reduce injustice and exploitation? The truth is that transforming individuals through the gospel and working for justice and humanity by social and political action must go hand in hand. The fight against slavery in the early nineteenth century, for example, included evangelistic activity that transformed slave owners and taught them that all men are equal before God. But it also involved intelligent political action by an evangelical group in the British Parliament for twenty years. To treat your slave as though he were your brother is a good start. But to abolish slavery is the proper Christian action, and that can only be done through political activity.

Secondly, we are to do God's will *as a whole*. We are highly skilled at picking and choosing which bits of God's will we are to observe. Think, for instance, of Jesus' last command in Matthew's Gospel, the command to make disciples among all peoples, to baptize them, and to 'teach them to obey *everything* I have commanded you' (Matthew 28: 19f). We don't mind making disciples and performing baptisms, but do we *really* treat all Jesus' teaching with the same seriousness – his teaching about money, about oppression of the poor, about revenge, about the meaning of love?

Thousands sing the *Magnificat* every Sunday, but how many allow its revolutionary message to motivate their thought and action? Sung by Mary the mother of Jesus before his birth, this song outlines the spiritual, social and economic changes which Jesus would bring:

> God 'shows mercy to all who fear him,
> From one generation to another.
> He stretched out his mighty arm
> And scattered the proud with all their plans.
> He brought down the mighty kings from their thrones,
> And lifted up the lowly.
> He filled the hungry with good things,
> And sent the rich away with empty hands' (Luke 1:50–53).

So sure is Mary that Jesus' coming will set this revolution in motion that she speaks as though it has already happened! And yet so often since the coming of Jesus the Church has been among those who resist social and economic change because of its own vested interests.

Thirdly, we must be involved in social change because it is taking place anyway whether we like it or not. But it often takes place without any clear guidelines, and guidelines are what Christians must seek to provide. For example, we split up communities by building motorways straight through them. But if man is created to live in community, that is a disastrous policy. The 1967 Abortion Act resulted in the widespread belief that unborn babies are disposable objects, the inconvenient products of thoughtlessness or bad luck, rather than potential human beings destined for eternity with God. The Christian truth about man provides guidelines by which we can decide what changes in society are desirable. We must declare them.

Fourthly, if we refuse to get involved we are compromising with evil because we are implicitly endorsing the *status quo*. When Martin Luther King led black protest in America many Christians labelled him a communist. When Christians react like that because their own position is threatened it is not surprising that many oppressed minorities resort to violence and revolution. If we claim that God's kingly rule is of first priority (Matthew 6: 33), then we dare not fail to speak and act about all manifestations of evil.

When Salome danced at Herod's birthday party and asked for the head of John the Baptist, Herod was not the only man guilty of murder that day. There were the guests − government officials, military chiefs and respectable citizens − who shared Herod's guilt because no one spoke out against the brutal injustice of it (Mark 6: 16–29). To say 'I didn't want to get involved' is no excuse. It is to condone evil. It is to regard your own comfort and safety more highly than the will of God. The day of judgment will be a day of condemnation for those who 'love only themselves and reject what is right, to follow what is wrong' (Romans 2: 8).

The fifth motive for social action is this. In the kingdom of God to which we look forward the will of God will be perfectly done. But since Jesus came the kingdom of God has already broken into history. Therefore those who belong to God's kingdom must do all they can to make God's will a reality *now*. We who pray, 'May your kingdom come, may your will be done on earth as it is in heaven' become the instruments through whom that prayer can be answered. We who long for God's kingdom of justice and peace, love and community must demonstrate the reality of the kingdom by working for these values in human society. The fact that we can never fully achieve them is beside the point: if we can achieve them at all we are promoting God's will for men. We are pointing to the nature of God's final kingdom, and at the same time we are showing that God's kingdom will never *fully* come until Jesus comes to end all opposition to his will.

The Church's role

The Church's task in all this is threefold. First, we have a *prophetic* function. We take our cue here from the Old Testament prophets as well as from Jesus himself. Isaiah warned the sophisticated women of Jerusalem, who lived in the lap of luxury at a time of national crisis (Isaiah 3: 16–4: 2). Amos rounded on the rich men of Israel:

'For crime after crime of Israel
I will grant them no reprieve,
because they sell the innocent for silver
and the destitute for a pair of shoes.
They grind the heads of the poor into the earth
and thrust the humble out of their way' (Amos 3: 6f).

'Can horses gallop over rocks?
Can the sea be ploughed with oxen?
Yet you have turned into venom the process of law
and justice itself into poison' (Amos 6: 12).

Jesus was incensed at seeing God's temple exploited for commercial gain. He declared judgment on religious leaders who 'take advantage of widows and rob them of their homes, then make a show of saying long prayers!' And he added, 'Their punishment will be all the worse!' (Luke 20: 47).

Sadly, you are more likely to find genuinely prophetic words in the *Daily Mirror* and the Left Wing protest movements than in the average church. But our role is to speak out, on national and local issues – and prepare to be unpopular.

Secondly, we are to be *politically active*. This doesn't mean that a church should commit itself to one particular political party – history shows the folly of that. But it is in politics that laws are passed and social policies thrashed out. Therefore Christians must be involved in politics, making Christian values known. The gospel is not politics, but there is a politics of the gospel – a message about injustice, the distribution of wealth, freedom of conscience, protection for minority groups, and so on. At the very least this means casting our vote for policies which will be for the general welfare of society, rather than for policies which are most likely to line our own pockets. For many of us it will mean more active involvement in politics than that. In any case we do well to remember James Baldwin's words: 'A civilization is not destroyed by wicked people: it is not necessary that people be wicked but only that they be spineless'.

Thirdly, we shall get nowhere unless we *practise what we preach*. It is easier to campaign for racial equality in South Africa than it is to love the coloured man who lives next door. We cannot protest about disregard of elderly people if we don't love them as part of the Christian fellowship. We have no right to denounce Britain's pathetically small contributions to development of the Third World if our church uses all its income to keep its own buildings in order.

But let's not be too timid to say what the Church has achieved. In India, for example, a significant proportion of nurses and teachers are Christians. Most of the pressure against the caste system has come from the churches – and the inequality between men which the caste system perpetuated was a major barrier to India's social and economic development. The need for adequately motivated teachers and the importance of equality among men are stressed by Gunnar Myrdal. His two books *Asian Drama* and *The Challenge of World Poverty* would do Christians more good than the diet of superficial 'Christian success-stories' on which many of us are hooked.

We must practise what we preach. If we aim for harmony between nations we must demonstrate a real international love in our Christian fellowship. If we condemn the affluence of the Western World in contrast to the poverty of the Third World, we must practise sacrifice and self-denial in the Church. It will not be easy, but we shall be working out God's will and so living as 'citizens of heaven'.

Plan for action

I have said that the Christian view of heaven provides guidelines which enables us to decide what our goals should be now. What will this mean in practice? Here are some brief examples.

First, we saw that God's new world will involve *the transformation of the natural world*. The earth will not simply be destroyed, it will be used up in the creation of something new. This gives us a motive for treating the earth with respect now. A mid-West American farmer who made his land into a dust-bowl by over-exploiting it remarked, 'Why should I think about posterity? Posterity never did anything for me'. But he wasn't just a selfish human being – he was a bad theologian! One reason, among others, why we should respect the environment and fight pollution is that this is God's earth for which he has further purposes in view. If we don't respect our environment now as we expect to respect our environment then, we are living as men without hope. And when Christ comes we shall be judged for our failure to be proper stewards of the world which he entrusted to us.

Secondly, heaven is a realm of *self-giving love*. How many problems can you think of in your locality where the only hope of a solution is in sacrificial, risk-taking love? Is there any other answer to the deadlock in Northern Ireland? I don't know, and it would be wrong for me to pontificate when I don't live there. But I do know this. History does not encourage us to believe that lasting solutions to national or personal feuds can be made through people *fearing* each other. Creative solutions only occur because someone is willing to make the first move and risk his own reputation, his own security in love for the other side. He may be regarded as crazy, he may be crucified. But beyond crucifixion lies hope of new beginnings.

Thirdly, heaven is a place of *community*. But if man is created for life in community, what on earth are we aiming at when we put people in high-rise flats where there is no sense of community, and in dehumanized working conditions where there is no possibility of community? If we believe that the most important things in life aren't things but relationships with people, why do we regard our obligations to our fellow-men as strictly material? Why, for example, do we think we've done our duty when we've footed the bill for an elderly relative to live in an institution or a lonely flat? A host of social problems arise because men's need for community is not taken seriously enough. The vision of God's kingdom can help to correct this.

Another characteristic of God's kingdom is *justice*. All God's people are equally precious to him, and in his kingdom there are no 'favourites', no vested interests. Here is a goal to aim at, a goal which at present is a long way off. Look for example at the distribution of the world's wealth and resources. Of course, it would be foolish to imagine that we can ever attain a perfectly equal distribution, an absolutely equal standard of living for every human being. It would be foolish too to imagine that the people of the Third World *want* the excessively materialistic kind of society we have created in the West. But let's not leave it at that – after all, when noises are made about the impossibility of making all men equal, they are usually made by rich men and nations who have their own vested interests to protect.

Consider the following facts. They are oversimplified through lack of space; they are just the tip of an ominous iceberg. A British person in his lifetime eats at least twenty times as much food as the average Indian. One in every three Americans is overweight, one in every five Britons. So while millions die of starvation in the developing countries, we in Britain spend £52 million a year on slimming pills and low calorie foods – quite apart from health hydros, massage parlours and countless other devices for helping us get our weight down. We feed our livestock on cheap imported protein: fish meal from Peru and Chile, linseed oil products from India and Africa – countries whose diets are notably short of protein, whose governments choose to feed their economies rather than their people. When we complain about increases in the price of tea or coffee, how many of us realize that the people who grow these foods in Sri Lanka and Brazil are paid barely enough to keep their families alive? And the respectable companies which are household names to us must take some of the blame for this.

The rich exploit the poor in all kinds of ways. Until the Zambian government banned Fanta Orange adverts in 1973, thousands of Zambian babies suffered from malnutrition because their mothers fed them on Coca-Cola and Fanta instead of milk. Mothers who genuinely wanted to do the best for their children were taken in by alluring adverts, and had no money left to buy real food. The *New Internationalist* regularly draws attention to such instances of 'the unacceptable face of capitalism'.

But what about the millions we give in aid to the developing countries? We aren't so generous as we sound. The United Nations have asked developed countries to give 0.7 per cent of their Gross National Products every year in development aid to the poor countries. Most – including Britain and the United States – have not achieved it. And even what we do give is no straightforward gift. Much of it is in the form of loans which have to be repaid with interest. More than half the world's aid is 'tied': that means we stipulate that the country receiving it must use it only to buy products from the country giving the aid. No wonder President Nixon said in 1968: 'Let us remember, the main purpose of American foreign aid is not to help other nations but to help ourselves' [J. McGinnis, *The Selling of the President*, 1970, p. 118]. We can commend him for his honesty, and deplore this assumption which lies behind so much apparent generosity. When you hear of Russia supplying snow-ploughs to tropical Guinea and someone sending a canning factory to the Sudan, where there's nothing to can, you realize how crazy the whole system is. But it's not just crazy, it's sinister. The whole set-up has the effect of *increasing* the gap between rich and poor.

So what can we do? Let's be clear about one thing: we're not talking about charity, we're talking about *justice*. The man who grows my coffee, the baby suffering from Coca-Cola and malnutrition – they are my brothers. They are as valuable in God's sight as I am. I have no more *right* to be healthy and comfortable than they have.

We have to choose – do we believe the third verse of 'All things bright and beautiful'? –

'The rich man in his castle,
The poor man at his gate,
God gave them all their station
And ordered their estate.'

Or do we take up the challenge of Helder Camara, Archbishop of Recife in Brazil? – 'True Christianity rejects the idea that some men are born poor and others rich and that the poor must attribute their poverty to the will of God, when it is injustices between men which are our real problem.'

We must get away from a flag-day approach. We must petition MPs and persuade our government to take decisive steps to restrain exploitation, and to make more positive contributions to world development. The Common Market is the world's richest trading block and could be giving a lead in all this. So far it seems more concerned to be a club for the rich.

There are about 800 million people living in conditions of absolute poverty, malnutrition and disease – conditions which make it very hard to be fully human. If their situation is to improve, we must demonstrate to affluent Western man that *his* 'true life is not made up of the things he owns, no matter how rich he may be' (Luke 12: 15). The economic cake can't go on for ever getting bigger, and if others are to get a slice at all, we must be willing to take a smaller slice. We must follow in practical ways the pattern set by Jesus in the spiritual realm: 'rich as he was, he made himself poor for your sake, in order to make you rich by means of his poverty' (2 Corinthians 8:9).

The gap between rich and poor nations is only one example of injustice. There are many others within our own society. To try to do anything about it may seem like trying to dig the Channel Tunnel with a pen-knife. But the feeling that we can achieve little is no reason for not doing what we can.

What chance of success?

Respect for the natural world, love, community, justice – these are some of the values which the Christian vision of heaven puts before us to aim at in human society. What chance is there that society will really come to reflect these values?

There is no chance of complete and final solutions this side of heaven. On the cornerstone of the United Nations building in New York are these words from Isaiah, chapter two: 'They shall beat their swords into plowshares, and their spears into pruning hooks; nation shall not lift up sword against nation, neither shall they learn war any more.' But this passage is about what will happen when the Messiah comes to transform God's world. While the United Nations may reduce conflict between nations, there will be no *ultimate* peace until Jesus comes again. There will be no *ultimate* answers to our other problems till then.

And yet there can be *partial* answers. If this is God's world, if his Spirit is at work in it, if prayer works and if love makes a difference, then surely we can expect to catch glimpses of God's kingdom on earth. Even though we know that we are 'strangers and pilgrims on the earth', we should do all we can to improve the conditions of men's lives. Why? Because love and justice and all the values which will be basic in heaven are God's will for men *now*.

The Church is to be a *sign* of God's kingdom, pioneering things which are God's will for men. That is what the

Church at its best has always been. Who pioneered mass education? Who pioneered hospitals? Who pioneered the abolition of slavery? In each case Christians played a leading role in causing progressive change. What are the issues today which the Church should be pioneering? If there has been progress in the past, there can be progress in future. As a pioneer of progress towards the will of God, the Church is a sign of the reality of God's kingdom.

The ultimate vision

And yet we know that the more we strive to achieve the values of the kingdom of God, the more we long to see them *perfectly* achieved at the coming of Jesus. If we have caught a glimpse of the love of God, we long to live closer to it. If we have experienced the work of the Holy Spirit in our lives, we long for the life of heaven to which it points. If we have learnt to hate evil, we look for the day when it will be finally overthrown. If we have learnt to love God's will, we long to see it perfectly done. Jesus, crucified and exalted, is the key to this hope. He is God's pledge that hope will not be disappointed.

But isn't hope of heaven selfish? No, it is desire for God, for his truth, for his will. If someone offered you the chance to spend a holiday with him at his expense, would you be selfish to accept? No – it would be ingratitude not to. But isn't it selfish to hope that Christ will come soon, when you have friends who are still unbelievers and will have no place in God's kingdom? That is a solemn thought. But the unbeliever cannot be allowed for ever to blackmail the universe – to deny for everyone else the final blessing of God's kingdom which he refuses to accept for himself.

No, your hope for the coming of Jesus is not selfish – if that very hope drives you to mission, to service and sacrificial love. Christian hope is quite different from escapism. It is hope which drives you into situations of conflict and squalor, of injustice and inhumanity – there to announce the kingdom of God and to live as subjects of the King.

But Christian hope is not mere wishful thinking. It is a hope that leads somewhere – to the triumph of God. As people who have heard God's loving invitation to share in his victory, we long for the day when the shout will be heard: 'Praise God! For the Lord, our Almighty God, is King! Let us rejoice and be glad; let us praise his greatness! For the time has come for the wedding of the Lamb, and his bride has prepared herself for it' (Revelation 19: 6f).

The time between now and then may be long or short – but that day *is* approaching.

'Tomorrow, and tomorrow, and tomorrow,
Creeps in this petty pace from day to day,
To the last syllable of recorded time.'

But that last syllable is the doorway to God's new beginning.

For further reading

*J. Gladwin, *God's People in God's World* (IVP, 1979)

B. Griffiths (ed.), *Is Revolution Change?* (IVP, 1972)

R. Sider, *Rich Christians in an Age of Hunger* (Hodder, 1978)

A. N. Triton, *Salt to the World* (IVP, 1979)

A. N. Triton, *Whose World?* (IVP, 1970)

New Internationalist, a monthly magazine sponsored by Oxfam and Christian Aid, from New Internationalist, Montagu House, High Street, Huntingdon, PE18 6EP.

Third Way, a monthly magazine offering a biblical perspective on current issues, from Third Way, 186 Kennington Park Road, London SE11.

Questions for Discussion

1. In what ways, if any, has British society moved closer to the ideal of the kingdom of God during the twentieth century?

2. How effectively does your church or group exercise the role of being prophetic, politically active and practising what it preaches?

3. Think of some exámples of worldwide, national or local injustice, and plan what your group can do about them.

4. Study Luke 1: 46–55. Mary rejoices in anticipation over several aspects of what Jesus is going to do. What are they? In what ways is Jesus doing these things today? Notice how the 'spiritual' and the 'social action' aspects of Christ's work are woven together, and discuss the implications of that for the Church today.